Nurturing Your Child's Inner Life

*Help Your Child Find Peace,
Harmony and Purpose*

Mary Ellen Maunz

Age of Montessori

NURTURING YOUR CHILD'S INNER LIFE
Help Your Child Find Peace, Harmony and Purpose
Copyright © 2012 Age of Montessori
All rights reserved

For information, contact
Age of Montessori
1103 Reeves Road West, Suite D
Bozeman, MT 59718 USA
www.ageofmontessori.org
406.284.2160

ISBN: 978-1-4751-6952-2

Photo credits: John Foxx/Stockbyte/Thinkstock, 17; Comstock/
Thinkstock, 37, 147, 167; iStockphoto/Thinkstock, 45, 54, 59,
93, 105, 113, 203; Ryan McVay/Lifesize/Thinkstock, 111; Digital
Vision/Thinkstock, 199; Jupiterimages/Comstock/Thinkstock, 214

In order to honor both male and female children, the author alternates
the use "he" and "she" when referring to a single child.

Contents

To the mothers in my life, who have inspired me and taught me so much.

To my children, who are my heroes, each of them, for their love, their integrity and their fiery spirits.

To the friends who have helped with the content and production of this book and who wrestled ideas with me: Tani, Randall, Holliday, Bradley, Deborah, Timothy and Colleen. To the kind first readers who have taken time from their busy lives to read the book and offer suggestions: Nancy, Jerome, Patti, Robin and Merrie. To my editors Peter, Neroli and Karen especially—I could not have done it without your loving and expert help.

Thank you!

Nurturing Your Child's
Inner Life

The real danger threatening humanity is the emptiness in men's souls; all the rest is merely a consequence of this emptiness.

—Maria Montessori

Introduction

The seed idea for this book was formed at six o'clock on a cool spring morning riding in a taxi from JFK Airport through the poverty-stricken areas of New York. I had taken a red-eye flight from Los Angeles to attend an educational conference in Tarrytown, and although I was exhausted and much in need of sleep, I was transfixed by the sight of block after block of dismal squalor. I pondered how living in this environment would limit a child's sense of what is possible in life.

In that moment I had a sudden realization. If I were the richest land developer in New York or the most powerful mayor of the city, I could raze this entire section of the city and rebuild it completely with beautiful buildings and beautiful gardens. But I knew that if the consciousness of the people did not change to include a larger, more beautiful sense of life, then the city would return to what it was now—the depression and hopelessness, the emptiness of soul that I saw around me.

The question was, how do you change the consciousness of the people? This question and the answers that began to percolate in my mind and in my heart were a turning point in my life. I knew that morning that teaching children was not enough. I also had to dedicate my life to working with parents, for parents hold the fate of their children in their hands.

No matter how much we as parents love our children and

want to help them, we cannot grow their inner lives for them. We still sometimes hinder them in the development and expression of their unique potential when we do not fully understand what they need. Even when we know what our children need, parenting is a very tough job. How often have I heard parents say, "It's hard to raise children today with all the influences of iPods, video games, violence on television and peer pressure at school! How can we foster the inner life when the culture we live in is all about money, sex, drugs and glamour?"

My experience in that taxi took place in 1978, but the clear memory of the feelings I experienced that morning has never left me. And while it has taken me thirty-three years working with children and their parents to feel ready to finally write about it, that experience was the initial impetus for this book about the inner life of your child.

The inner life

Nurturing the inner lives of our children offers them the opportunity to connect with a deeper part of themselves. This deeper connection fills their souls with hope and love rather than the emptiness of soul that endangers our world.

When I speak of the inner life in this book, I am referring to something deeper, something joyful, more profound than everyday thoughts and feelings. When I stand in awe of a beautiful sunset and feel a surge of joy rippling through me or when I have an inner knowing that a big project I am ready to tackle is the right thing for me, this experience transcends thought and feeling. These are moments when I feel the contact with the depth of my inner life as well as something much larger than myself.

I have asked many people to share with me their definitions of the inner life. Among my favorites are those definitions from two of my own children. My youngest is a courageous, talented and beautiful young woman who has faced multiple life-and-death medical challenges. She told me very simply, "To me, the inner life is peace. It is that place you can go to get through the tough things. It has to do with being able to sleep at night, being comfortable in your skin. I don't always have it but I know it is there."

She went on to share with me how my constant support for her life and the guidance to go in the right direction with the freedom to make her own decisions have given her the sense of the reality of her inner life and of her own inner teacher. "You have always been there to support me, no matter what, and this has given me the confidence that I can do anything."

My older daughter, also immensely talented, beautiful and a childhood cancer survivor, told me that to her the inner life is the private part of herself, the essence of who she is. She said, "The inner life has spiritual connotations for me. It is the wellspring that drives me forward. It is what I can tap into for inspiration. It also refers to my mental life and the ability to think through things deeply and carefully so I know what to do next. It is where I find connections between things, new interests and the desire to explore." She commented that when I first asked her about the inner life she was thinking about it from the perspective of being an adult, but then she realized it is also "the child's incredible creativity to express what is inside of her and not just what she outwardly sees."

The themes of inspiration, joy and inner guidance came up repeatedly in people's descriptions of the inner life.

The need for wholeness

Every child has a physical body, a mind, emotions and a spirit, however we may define it. If a child has a physical need, such as food or play, we feed him and let him run outside. If he has emotional needs and wants a hug, we give him a hug. If he needs a book to read because he wants to learn, we give him a book.

But what about the spiritual needs of the child? What are they? Do we even recognize them when they arise? And how do we meet them? I wrote this book to address these questions. Even more importantly, what happens when our educational system and even many of our homes ignore the spirit within the child?

If the spiritual needs of children are neglected, their spiritual natures do not develop in parallel with their mental, emotional and physical abilities. And when this fundamental integration in the lives of children is missing, they grow up and an entire society may then suffer from a lack of integration.

When we have a society that lacks integration of the inner life with the outer life, there is, as Maria Montessori said, an emptiness in people's souls. Without integration, there is the absence of wholeness, the absence of integrity—qualities that are so needed in the world today, whether in in government or business or in the personal lives of public and private figures.

For this to change, we need to seriously reconsider not only how we nurture our children's connection to a rich inner life, but also how we educate our children in a larger sense. We have to tackle the very meaning of education and shift it from the concept of pouring in to the concept of a release from within. The original meaning of education comes from the Latin *educare,* meaning to lead out from within.

I have observed again and again that children have a deep and rich spiritual life which unfolds in an entirely natural way if it is fostered and nurtured. Here are two examples.

I was in Russia, on the Black Sea, in 2004. It was my first of many trips there, and some friends had gotten together and invited me to speak with their children, ages 6 to 12. I began talking about the spirit within and about our opportunity to grow and fulfill the mission that each of us came to do. It was a simple message, and my heart was full as I spoke with them through an interpreter. One of the boys, who was about 10 years old, looked at me and said, "This is for me!" His eyes were simply shining with this understanding of the possibilities of life. At that moment, I felt that it had been worth travelling all the way to Russia just for this one child.

Several years ago, I was teaching a group of children in an upper elementary Montessori classroom. I worked very hard to make this classroom a place where the children had many choices and the opportunity to explore what was of special interest to them. Together we created a lovely community within this classroom. One of our favorite classroom rituals was a "show and share" segment each Friday when the children had the opportunity to bring something from home that they wanted to show their classmates.

This is a very common school activity, but on this special morning it was anything but common. A girl in fourth grade came to class with a beautiful leather-bound book, which I thought was what she was going to show the other children. But inside the book, she had written a song and she wanted to sing it as her contribution to the class.

Swooping in the Air
By Clara

Some days I watch the birds fly over me.
Some days I wish I could fly like the birds
And feel the glory of joy sweep over me
And gather in my heart.
Suddenly I rise up
And a smile comes on my face.

Then I swoop into the air
And as the sun shines on me
The blue sky above spreads over me.
And I swoop into the clouds
And look down at all the things below me
And wave to everything I see.

And then I come down and back to my house.
And as I lay in my bed
I'm filled with thoughts of joy.

I was moved that this little girl wrote such a beautiful song and even more moved that she was willing to share it with her classmates in a solo performance. It was a testimony to the community we had built together that she felt that this was something that she could do. I thought of the many classrooms I have seen in my life, including where I went to school, where a child would never feel safe enough do something like that.

The response of the other children was also revealing. They were silent at first and then broke into spontaneous applause. Some of them got up and hugged her. It was a precious moment for all as this child revealed something of her inner self.

The child's approach to spirituality has its own special

characteristics at each stage of development. In this book we will explore these characteristics and how we can nurture our child's inner life each step of the way.

Spirituality and religion

As we begin to explore the inner life of the child, it is helpful to think about the difference between spirituality and religion. According to author Paul Beyers, spirituality refers to asking and honoring the great questions we all have about life and why we are here on earth. Religion refers to the set of answers to these questions that a particular belief system offers its followers.[1]

Spirituality is the strength of our connection with the creative force of the universe, with the inner light, with eternal principles, with universal Law. It is the depth of our love for life, for God and for man. It is the spontaneity of the child's desire to know about the world and about life.

To truly nurture their inner lives, children need to have direct *experiences* of that inner life—not just mere words about it. According to the authors of a book titled *Conscious Education:*

> This deep connection to creation evolves over our entire life. It may be experienced as special moments when one is alone in the forest, or when one stares into the heavens on a star-filled night, or observes cloud formations. It is an experience of awe and wonder and an awareness of the oneness of all. Spirituality is the recognition of the inherent beauty, truth and goodness in life. It calls forth such traits as compassion, joy and humility.[2]

The difference between spirituality and religion is at the heart of one challenge I faced when writing this book. I know that many readers who desire to nurture the inner lives of their children are deeply religious and would want me to speak about God in terms that they are familiar with. I also know that some readers may not follow any particular religion, and some may even be uncomfortable with references to God.

In this book, I have tried to meet the needs of both groups: to speak about the inner life and the spirit, and also the child's tie to God. The inner life is strong and real in every child, no matter what words we may use to identify it. I simply offer the meditation of my heart to you for the nurturing of your child in the way you wish to do it and according to whatever spiritual path or tradition you follow.

Therefore, we will explore how to nurture the inner life of the child rather than how to teach a particular religion. Many of the suggested activities will work for someone of any faith. Some of the lessons and activities are based on Christianity, while others are based on other world religions. Even if these are not your path, in our increasingly ecumenical world it is valuable to gain an understanding of how our brothers and sisters around the world live and worship. Children themselves love to learn about the ways other children live.

Whatever belief system you may have, the lessons and exercises can be easily adapted to that path, since they utilize simple educational principles of action and interest. I will consistently point in the direction of proposing experiences for your child that will deepen his or her inner life.

Children are natural philosophers

A wise teacher once told me that children are natural philosophers. When you stop to think of it, it is so clearly true! Every day children ask such profound questions. "Why is the sky blue?" "Why is the sun hot?" These are questions of cosmic magnitude.

One of my own children used to pose the most difficult theological questions to me. She wanted the whole cosmic design: "Why did God make the world?"

This was not just a random question. She really wanted an answer that would satisfy her hunger to understand. This question was something she would ask me again and again in many different ways, never quite having received enough to satisfy her desire to understand such a cosmic concept. These questions lasted from age 4 to early adulthood, in an ever more refined manner. They opened the door to many long, interesting discussions about life.

Sometimes these profound questions are triggered by circumstances in life. When a beloved pet dog dies or a grandparent dies, children will ask quite honestly and sincerely, often in a group setting, "What happens when we die?" After 9/11 a child in my school asked if God hated the world. She was grappling with the concept of evil.

Children who ask these questions are not trying to put us on the spot. They just want to know. They are showing us that their minds and hearts are open to the big questions, to the spiritual questions of life, and they are immensely curious. If we respect this longing and are open to these questions ourselves, we may be amazed and delighted with the sweet and vivid inner lives our children share with us.

When the big questions arise, it is important to talk about them when the interest is there, and not put them off to a later, more convenient time. Depending on your own beliefs and the age of the child, these questions may provide the perfect opportunity to share simple overall statements of your faith. When the questions are difficult, you may wish to share your wondering with your child, letting him or her know that these are questions people all over the world have pondered since the beginning of time. You may feel comfortable with a clear and concise answer based on your theology, or you can choose to be with the child in the awe and wonder of the universe.

Sometimes a simple answer is all that is needed and sometimes the child is seeking more. She may want to talk about what has happened in her life and may be seeking to make sense of it. If you observe your child's reactions, you will learn which aspects of your response, and perhaps even which face of God, resonates within her. You don't have to be an expert theologian or give the perfect answer, but just speak honestly from your heart.

Generally speaking, less is more. If you try to teach too much you may bore your child or even confuse him. The simpler, more essential your answer, the more satisfying it will be. If you give just enough to satisfy him and leave him wanting more, you can leave the door open for the time when the child asks for more or you wish to give more.

Sometimes words simply do not and cannot capture the vastness of inner spiritual experiences. And the child is perhaps even more capable than we of direct experience of the spirit, so we want to make certain we are not prematurely closing off the meditations of their hearts with formulaic answers.

Ultimately these are all questions about the natural laws

of life. There are many ways we can point out the cycles of existence in everyday moments. When a flower dies, its seeds fall to the ground and next year new plants emerge. Every spring we celebrate new birth as cycles of life bring daffodils and blossoms of all kinds.

Life is not random, but constructs itself according to patterns. Walking in the garden you see a sunflower. The hundreds of seeds follow a golden-ratio spiral, the geometric progression that governs plant growth, seashell design, classical architecture and even the human body.

Sitting by a still pond you toss a pebble and watch the ripples. Our actions and our words cause similar ripples among those we interact with—the more kindness we send out, the more kindness will return.

It is not the intent of this little book to try to provide answers for the immense questions of life. Our individual belief systems and the theology we subscribe to will guide us in this. The intent is rather to acknowledge and better understand the powerful force of the spirit within the child that seeks both questions and answers as well as the freedom to express itself.

The seeds in the sunflower follow the pattern of the golden-ratio spiral

We will explore ways in which we can nurture the inner lives in our children from conception onward and teach them to honor the flame of life in all of its vital and amazing manifestations. Using examples drawn from both universal principles and specific scriptural teaching, we will see how we can take a very big idea and break it into smaller, manageable pieces. Using these principles, you will see how you can create simple activities for your children that will make these ideas come alive.

Maria Montessori

In forty years as an educator I have studied and applied the principles of Dr. Maria Montessori, three-time nominee for the Nobel Peace Prize, the first woman doctor in Italy and perhaps the most famous educator of the twentieth century. Maria Montessori lived from 1870 to 1952. After extensive work with mentally handicapped children, in 1907 she started a school for normal children. That first school has spread to tens of thousands of schools all over the world. Montessori schools everywhere honor the inner teacher of the child, that direct link to the inner life that affords children the opportunity to manifest their true spiritual nature. That inner tie also leads to academic and creative excellence.

I have had the immense privilege of teaching hundreds of children from 2 to 12 with the Montessori Method of education and I have trained Montessori teachers on four continents. This service has afforded me the opportunity to observe children in their homes and schools in many different cultures, and I have seen how the Montessori Method supports the development of the whole child—physically, mentally, emotionally and spiritually.

The reason I choose to work in the field of Montessori education is simply that my heart leapt when I read her words and saw her principles at work. This is a method of education, practiced in homes and schools around the world, that recognizes and nurtures the child's spontaneous developmental impulses, offers constructive choice and fosters the deep concentration that puts children in touch with their inner teacher. I have seen that with repeated inner experiences, children develop the habit of following the direction of the inner teacher, the higher self—which some think of as the voice of conscience, the inner knowing of the right thing to do in any situation.

The Montessori Method, in and of itself, nurtures the inner life of the child. Montessori was very aware of this. She simply said, "Nothing is done if we do not liberate the spirit."[3]

In my years in the field of education, I have also had the opportunity to study with Dr. Sofia Cavalletti, pioneer in the application of Montessori's principles to the field of spiritual education.

These two women, from their combined experience of more than a hundred years working with children, came to understand that the spiritual life of the child is profoundly different from the spiritual life of the adult. Childhood is more than a transition to adulthood. There is value in the child not only for the adult he will become, but also as he is, in a state of constant transformation and creativity.

A vital component of that value is the child's effect on adults. Montessori writes about the love that parents feel for their children, which can "annihilate selfishness and awaken the spirit of sacrifice.... The love which then begins is like a revelation of the moral greatness of which man is capable."[4]

The application of these principles to the inner life of

the spirit, as originally proposed by Maria Montessori and developed by Sofia Cavalletti, was brilliant in concept and scope. The child is one whole being. We cannot separate the child's spirit from his mind, his feelings or his body. In fact, activities that are self-chosen based on personal interests and desires, which require thought to complete and incorporate physical activity—all Montessori hallmarks—allow the perfect integration of heart, head and hand. They allow the child to be at peace and focus on his work, which *is* self-development.

With a little forethought, everything we do to set free the child in the home and classroom environment can contribute toward his spiritual liberation and his contact with his inner teacher, the spiritual guiding force inside him. Perhaps we sometimes think that the more we do for our children the more we demonstrate our love. Maria Montessori reminds us, however, that everything we do for the child that he can do for himself is an obstacle to his development.

It is a novel way of thinking to regard the child's inner independence as something to be encouraged and honored. But as much as we love our children, we cannot develop their inner lives for them any more than we can grow their teeth for them. We can only make certain they have the time, space and nurturing to explore the riches within.

Maria Montessori wrote:

> If education is always to be conceived as a mere transmission of knowledge, there is little to be hoped from it in the bettering of man's future. For what is the use of transmitting knowledge if the individual's total development lags behind?...
>
> The child is endowed with unknown powers, which

can guide us to a radiant future. If what we really want is a new world, then education must take as its aim the development of these hidden possibilities.[5]

What I have sought to do in this book is to show that nurturing your child's inner life and spirituality is as natural as breathing. Anyone can do it—parents, teachers and all who interact with children. Rich opportunities occur every day in our homes, families, schools and communities. All we need to do is observe life, take advantage of the opportunities it presents for us to model and teach, and allow the little child to lead us.

When we nurture the inner lives of our children, we will find that not only will they be immeasurably enriched, but so will we.

1

The Inner Teacher
and the Divine Plan

If a child has within himself the key to his own personality, if he has a plan of development, and laws to be observed, these must be delicate powers indeed, and an adult by his untimely interventions can prevent their secret realization.

From time immemorial men, through their interference with these natural laws, have hindered the divine plan for children and, as a consequence, God's plan for men themselves.

—Maria Montessori

Wayne Dyer, noted author and lecturer, once told a story that gives insight into the spiritual life of children. There was a young family with two children—a four-year-old girl and a new baby. The older child repeatedly begged to be left alone with the newborn. The mother and father, thinking of stories they had heard about sibling rivalry and the possibility that the older child might try to hurt the newborn, didn't think this was a good idea.

But the little girl persisted. It eventually dawned on the parents that they had a baby monitor in the room where the baby slept. So the next time the four-year-old asked to be alone with her sister, they agreed to her request. They left her alone in the bedroom with the baby with the intercom switched on.

The parents strained to hear the quiet voice of the child whispering to her baby sister, "Tell me about God, I'm starting to forget."

There is something about this story that touches us. Where does such a question come from? What a precious sense of spiritual awareness the little four-year-old is so eager to keep alive within herself!

This inner life is very much alive in all young children, although we don't always see it, perhaps because we have not known to look for it. What do we do about it in our homes and churches? How can we nurture the spiritual life of our children? When Jerome Berryman, author of *Young Children and Worship,* was in his middle year at Princeton Theological Seminary, he was dismayed to find that children were scarcely mentioned. Even in a required religious education class, adult education was the primary focus, and there was very little about the religious education of children—and even that seemed superficial. He writes about his experience:

> Children were treated like empty vessels that needed entertaining and filling up. The emphasis was on getting the doctrine right and then getting children to believe it. No one seemed to think that children might already know God and that what they needed was an appropriate language to construct their own personal meaning about that reality.[1]

Berryman's experience was that children have a personal knowledge of God. What was needed was a language to identify and express their experience with God and thereby have a means to integrate it with their outer awareness.

After working for ten years to develop a program based on his ideas, Berryman found in the Montessori Method the framework he was looking for. He moved his family to Italy for a year to study Montessori education and spent the next twenty years using these principles to develop a spiritual education program he called "Godly Play."

Jerome Berryman found that the Montessori Method was conducive to revealing the inner spirit. Maria Montessori explained her method with these simple words: "I observed little children; I sensed their needs; I tried to fulfill them: they call that the Montessori Method."

The method includes a prepared educational environment where children can live and work in freedom and peace. Maria Montessori's keen observations of children and her astute insights into how children learn enabled her to develop an environment of child-sized rich learning materials that answer the needs of the child's emerging developmental impulses. Even when it is not overtly spiritual, the deep, centered concentration that children engage in when they work leads them to connect with the spirit within. They reveal this connection with the joy and calm that they feel.

Montessori saw with the eyes of the heart. She consistently worked to put dignity within the reach of every child. As a physician, her heart went out to children who were considered to be deficient and uneducable and who were confined to institutions in Rome. She worked with them using hands-on materials that she developed and within one school year, many of them passed the state exams, surpassing many of their so called "normal" peers.

The application of these same techniques to large groups of average children, first in Rome and eventually all over the world, unlocked previously unseen and unrecognized potential. Montessori experimented with and created learning materials to facilitate the child's spontaneous learning. She observed that when allowed to freely choose materials in a carefully prepared environment, each child will select what he needs when he needs it.

With the opportunity to work for extended periods of time in peace and with full concentration, children become calm and joyful. They learn with ease through their interaction with the environment rather than through the words of the teacher. The fruits of an excellent Montessori program are children who love learning and are fully engaged in their own self-development both at home and at school.

Allowing the child to make these choices provides the opportunity for the child to exercise free will guided by the inner teacher. This kind of environment makes it possible for the child to be in touch with his own inner spirit and to become familiar with the voice of his own conscience rather than always relying on the external voice of authority to tell him what to do and what not to do. As the child learns to exercise free will constructively in these very early years, a sound foundation is laid for the exercise of free will in ever larger areas of responsibility as the child grows into the teenage years and beyond.

You can create a prepared environment that will nurture your child's inner life wherever you are—in your home, in your school, in your community or at church. Maria Montessori wrote in *Education and Peace,* "Man must be educated to realize his greatness and to become worthy of the powers that are his."[2] The inner life of the child is indeed a powerful force.

Children with a strong foundation in the inner life are more confident, more centered, and better equipped to deal with the challenges that life will inevitably bring. We will see in the chapters ahead how we can help our children develop that inner strength and awareness of beauty in life, no matter what the outer circumstances may be.

The divine blueprint within

Perhaps the most significant finding of Maria Montessori is that the child develops and grows because of the creative force and the divine blueprint within him, not because the adult teaches him. Following the direction and timeline of what

Maria Montessori called the "inner teacher," young children learn complex new skills without being taught.

In their very early years, children adapt to the culture in which they live and they learn the language of their people. No matter where in the world a child is born or what language she is learning, the process of learning to talk is the same. It makes no difference whether the language is relatively simple or highly complex. The child starts to babble, says single words and then phrases, and finally speaks in complete sentences. We don't sit down and teach our children how to talk, nor do we teach the rules of grammar, syntax and word order. Young children *absorb* language according to an internal timetable of development.

All over the world, children learn to walk. They creep, they crawl, they pull themselves upright, they take a few tentative steps. The process is the same anywhere, and although children may be encouraged by adults, they learn it by themselves when they are physiologically ready.

Children do not need to be taught these new skills, but they do need an environment in which they can be developed. The inner teacher selects from the environment what the child needs for each stage of development, revealing a self-directed individual who unfolds and blossoms in accordance with hidden directives.

When the child is preparing to speak, his ear inclines to the human voice. He must have access to the spoken word if he is to develop spoken language. When the child is preparing to walk, he must have the freedom of movement to allow him to creep, crawl and pull himself upright.

It is interesting to note that in addition to the fundamental needs of walking and talking, children have very definite preferences for what attracts them to develop their own unique

This 4-year-old had a strong affinity to music, and after he learned to play simple tunes on a set of bells, he learned about writing music with this lovely material of putting the notes on the staff.

This little girl was attracted to color and spent many happy hours sorting colors and grading these color tablets. She became so proficient with color she could look at one tablet, visualize its hue, and from memory find something in the classroom that matched almost exactly.

selfhood. One child is attracted to colors and drawing, while another likes geography and maps. Another child is attracted to geometric shapes and building, while another is fascinated by sounds and learns music.

Why does each child select different materials? Montessori explains that it is not an automatic process, but rather one guided from within by innate traits.

Where do the child's inherent characteristics come from? Are they gifts from God, part of the child's genetic inheritance, derived from patterns of early experience, or perhaps even soul momentums from previous lives?

Philosophers and mystics have presented their own answers to this question. I will simply share my own personal story of how these deep-seated interests can be so different, even in one family, and how we can so easily make unwarranted assumptions because of our own set of experiences.

I grew up playing with toy cars with my brother—our father sold cars, which was probably a large part of their attraction for me. When I became a parent myself, I assumed that all young children would love cars, as I had, and I got some toy cars for my firstborn son as soon as he was old enough. He was not the least bit interested. All he wanted to play with were toy animals and soldiers, and he loved to create art. My second child was not interested in either cars or animals, but loved to play with dolls. My third was a builder and creator of interesting two- and three-dimensional spaces. I had to throw aside my preconceived ideas and learn how to parent each one, attempting to provide what was most appealing to their highly individual interests.

Here's how Maria Montessori explains choice as an internal self-guided process:

> There is in man a special attitude to external things, which forms part of his nature, and determines its character. The internal activities act as cause; they do not react and exist as the effect of external factors. Our attention is not arrested by all things indifferently, but by those which are congenial to our tastes. The things which are useful to our inner life are those which arouse our interest. Our internal world is created upon

a selection from the external world, acquired for and in harmony with our internal activities. The painter will see a preponderance of colors in the world; the musician will be attracted by sounds. It is the quality of our attention which reveals ourselves, and we manifest ourselves externally by our aptitudes; it is not our attention which creates us.[3]

We choose what we wish to do and become because of who we are, not the other way around. We are not, as psychologist B. F. Skinner suggested, mere stimulus-response animals. A stimulus-response animal has no free will and no real initiative, but simply responds to whoever and whatever is feeding it information and experience.

However, when you watch children over a period of forty years as Maria Montessori did, and as I have had the amazing opportunity to do, you see that Skinner was not right. All three-year-olds are not alike—even when they are raised in an identical environment. All four-year-olds are not alike. They come bearing their own unique selfhood.

This selfhood tentatively peeping out is fragile, and it needs our loving help to fully emerge. Harsh words, constant interruptions or corrections as well as lack of stimulation can hold it back. It is our job as parents and educators to help each child expand the fullness of the potential of who he or she really is—not to fulfill our own ideal of what each should become.

The characteristics of the child

While each child is unique, we also see common characteristics of all children, which have to do with the natural stages of the unfolding of that unique potential. Some people think of the characteristics of the child as capriciousness, naughtiness and an inability to concentrate. Maria Montessori discovered just the opposite—self-discipline, a love of order and ability for intense focus and concentration.

She once wrote of her discovery of this abundance of riches within the inner life of the child:

> I set to work like a peasant woman who, having set aside a good store of seed corn, has found a fertile field in which she may freely sow it. But I was wrong. I had hardly turned over the clods of my field, when I found gold instead of wheat: the clods contained a precious treasure. I was not the peasant I had thought myself. Rather I was like foolish Aladdin, who, without knowing it, had in his hand a key that would open hidden treasures.[4]

These are the treasures that Montessori found when she provided an environment that supported the developmental needs of the child:

- Amazing mental concentration on activities that correspond to inner developmental needs
- Self-discipline when allowed to work for sustained periods of time on engaging activities
- Love of repetition of activities that integrate action and interest
- Love for order in the environment and the capacity to sustain order—they are very happy to put their own work away

- Ability to choose wisely from among constructive choices
- Love of silence
- Sense of personal dignity
- Preference of work over play—children will always prefer an activity that corresponds to developmental needs rather than mere entertainment
- Indifference to rewards and punishment—internal motivation is more important than external motivation
- Intense interest in writing and reading between the ages of 4 and 5

These characteristics give us pause. They are largely the opposite of what people often think of children! Yet we see them emerge in Montessori schools the world over. Montessori described these qualities as "more precious than gold, for they are man's own spirit."[5]

If we are not seeing these characteristics in the child, maybe there is more we can do to create an atmosphere conducive to their development. Perhaps we unconsciously hold back the child with our judgments. Could it be that we do not yet hold the vision of what the child has the potential to become? Unless we know there is something different from the impulsive and often unruly behavior we see in some settings, it is hardly surprising that we think that what we see now is all we will ever get.

In Montessori's writings, the explanation for why these natural characteristics of the child are not always apparent is quite simple. The child who does not show these characteristics has not yet been "normalized." Normalization occurs when the child comes into consonance with his deeper nature. This takes place through sustained concentration on external activities that correspond with the child's inner development. These periods of concentration, or this work, put the child in touch with his inner teacher and allow the inner life to connect with the external life.

Normalized children still have bad days, they will still act naughty and get riotously excited from time to time, and they may still try our patience to the uttermost. Children are children and we would not want it any other way. Yet when they have found a link to their own inner world, this brings great joy and peace and an unexpected calmness for sustained periods of time.

Many issues of fussiness and defiance come from the child who is somehow unable to follow or is not in touch with what his inner teacher needs him to do. The solution to this can be as simple as noting when some spontaneous interest arises and trying to support it, even if it does not make sense to you.

Sensitive periods and the laws of development

To better understand these spontaneous interests, it is helpful to know something of the "sensitive periods" in the development of all children. During a sensitive period the child experiences a deep longing to do certain activities.

These sensitive periods, originally observed by Dr. Montessori, have been identified in recent years by neuroscientists as stages when the brain is in need of specific kinds of stimulation in order to fully develop. One common example is a child who wants to walk on the curb or the cracks of the sidewalk. His inner need is to coordinate movement. If your child is in this sensitive period, find a quiet street and go for walks each day so your child gets lots of practice doing what his development requires. The child will lose interest in the activity when the internal development has adequately taken place.

A friend shared with me another example of a sensitive period. Her three-year-old daughter came into the bathroom to watch mom fix her hair. A little bowl of bobby pins sitting on the vanity table suddenly attracted the child's attention. She picked up the bowl and spilled the contents onto the floor. The mother admitted that her first reaction was to slap her daughter's hand and say, "No!" But she decided to watch and wait instead.

The little girl sat on the floor and picked up each bobby pin with her thumb and first finger and put it back in the bowl. Then she poured them all out and picked them up again. She repeated the entire process twice more, replacing the bowl carefully on the vanity when she had finished. Then she smiled sweetly at her mother and ran out to play. For the next two weeks, the child repeated the ritual each day. One day it was over, and she did not need to do it again.

What is happening here? The child was in the midst of a sensitive period for developing the pincer grip, that special coordination of movement of the thumb and fingers that will

This child is practicing a simple but engaging activity to gain mastery with the pincer grip.

allow her to hold a pencil when the time comes to write. The same skill is also used in more precise types of manipulations such as stringing beads and cutting with scissors.

Although the most prominent sensitive periods occur from birth to 6, there is a powerful sensitive period for acquiring culture in the elementary age period from 6 to 12.

I well remember myself at age 8. I became interested in butterflies. I was out with my net catching them and mounting them for days on end. It was a passion, a sensitive period to learn and organize information.

My brother and I spent hours on the roof of our walk-out garage, where we found the most monarchs and an occasional swallowtail. I got books from the library to learn the names of the different butterflies, I did a report at school on butterflies. I utilized this same sensitive period to gather and organize information about seashells and whales, to name two other examples of my own childhood passions.

To this day, I still love the beauty of butterflies. Just recently I captured a photo at a butterfly garden exhibit at the Museum of Natural History in Santa Barbara. Even after all these years, it was a real treat for me to see a swallowtail up close. This example of a sensitive period illustrates how the

interests of the child translate into the interests and capacities of the adult. Among my greatest interests and professional skills remains learning and ordering information.

We cannot predict precisely when the day will come for a particular sensitive period to begin, but there are general timetables that most children follow. One of the keys to your child's spiritual growth is understanding and anticipating these periods and knowing how to provide something in the environment that allows her to exercise what her spirit, her brain and her body want and need to accomplish.

If the little girl with the bobby pins had her hand slapped and not been allowed to touch the small objects calling to her, she might have recoiled and decided not to respond to her inner teacher. A step in her own development might have been missed, and such gaps in development may have far-reaching effects. I have taught a number of six-year-olds who could not hold a pencil correctly. In some cases they had not been allowed to handle small items when they were younger or there was nothing available in their environment at the time they needed it.

The genius of Maria Montessori was to observe these sensitive periods and to create an environment that provides literally dozens of little lessons that encourage the child to utilize the power of the sensitive periods to full advantage.

A particular activity attracts the child because it offers an external activity that corresponds to what the inner teacher is seeking to master, whether it is coordination of movement or care for nature. A child may repeat an activity, as the little girl with the bobby pins did, until some mysterious inner urge is satisfied and the child moves on to other sensitive periods. The inner self is nurtured and satisfied through these simple tasks.

These children are happily engrossed in activities they have freely chosen for themselves.

Integration of heart, head and hand

The child's choice of activity based on sensitive periods is a natural, deep process. This is not under the conscious control of the child but is directed by the inner teacher. When the child finds in the environment what he needs at the exact time he is ready to develop a new facet of self, we see harmonious and relatively steady growth—and often unexpected progress and mastery. We see calmness, joy and expansion of capacity. The child blossoms in response to delicate hidden directives. His work is like a spiritual meditation.

When we witness these moments of utter concentration, we are moved to realize that the spirit of the child is completely absorbed in his work. The child has chosen to block out distractions and to focus entirely on the work, unaware that he is constructing himself—the man he is to become—out of his tireless labor. But when we understand this simple concept, our respect for the humble tasks of the child grows.

Each activity integrates the child's heart, head and hand through his desire to do the lesson (heart), the mental activity required (head) and the physical action to complete the activity (hand) that allows the child to follow a sequence of steps and to learn fundamental concepts such as color, shape, and sound. This integration also opens the way to more complex learning such as how to read and write and do the four operations in math of addition, subtraction, multiplication and division.

Encouragement and acceptance from the adults in a child's life is a key element to the harmonious unfolding of the stages of development. If, however, the stimulus to develop is not met with encouragement or suitable environmental activities, we often see tantrums and delayed progress. It causes great conflict in the life of a child when the inner teacher is guiding him to a certain activity in order to grow, but the adults in his life do not understand what is happening within him and the activities he needs are not available.

Montessori reminds us in her usual clear and direct style:

Is there not within the child himself a power which enables him to save himself? It is this force, for instance, which leads him to touch things in order to become acquainted with them, and we say to him, "Do not touch"; he moves about to establish his equilibrium and we tell him to "keep still"; he questions us to acquire knowledge, and we reply, "Do not be tiresome." We relegate him to a place at our side, vanquished and subdued, with a few tiresome playthings.... He might well think: Why does she, whom I love so dearly, want to annihilate me?[6]

We see the truest fruits of the child's inner life when we prepare an environment rich in activities that are appropriate to the developmental level of the child and which leave the child free to select his work from among these activities. In this way, the child learns to follow the directives of his inner teacher, and he develops self-confidence and the habit of following his conscience.

Montessori saw that what she had learned about children in their everyday classroom experiences was a direct parallel to what she saw of their spiritual development. She felt, in fact, that nurturing the inner life of the child was the true end of the methods she had discovered.

The child is our teacher

The important point to remember is that the laws of development within the child are different from the laws of adult functioning. The child is in a constant stage of transformation and will accomplish more in the first three years of life than we adults can accomplish in decades. Adults, on the other hand, are more in the mode of consolidating what they have already developed. When adults are not fully aware of these differences, they may not understand their children and expect them to think and learn in the same way that adults do. This can only lead to frustration for both parents and children.

However, when we learn to understand and work with these differences, children and adults can enrich each other's lives and learn from one another. Montessori wrote:

The child and the adult are two distinct parts of humanity which must work together and interpenetrate

with reciprocal aid. Therefore it is not only the adult who must help the child, but also the child who must help the adult.[7]

The child brings us to the heights of love, and the inner life of the child can be our greatest inspiration. To the extent that we are receptive, we can learn much from the little child. Montessori wrote in *The Child in the Church* of the importance of learning about the laws governing the child's inner life.

God has given to the child a nature of his own and has fixed certain laws for his development, as much and as surely in the psychic realm [the realm of the soul] as in that of the physical. Anyone who is responsible for the child's normal development should become acquainted with those laws. To turn away from them would mean to lose that direction which God, as the guide of the child, gives us....

To discover the laws of the child's development would be the same thing as to discover the Spirit and

Wisdom of God operating in the child.... This is the true mentality for the educator—that is, the recognition of the Divine Wisdom as a necessary element in his work as an educator.[8]

Whether you believe in God or have another way of referring to these internal laws that exist in the heart of the child, we need to learn about them so that we can best support our children's overall development.

2

Stages of Development

*To everything there is a season, and a
time to every purpose under the heaven.*
—Ecclesiastes 3:1

*Successive levels of education must
correspond to the successive personalities of
the child.*
—Maria Montessori

Joan Wester Anderson documented many stories of the spiritual experiences of children in her book *An Angel to Watch Over Me: True Stories of Children's Encounters with Angels.* She writes:

> Most children have a sense of the sacred from their first days on earth.... We might say that young children have one foot in heaven and one on the earth, and for a little while they can be part of both worlds.
>
> An alert adult will notice evidence of this other dimension—infants who seem to be staring at something no one else can see, toddlers lifting their arms up to be held by an unknown someone, four- and five-year-olds playing very seriously with imaginary companions. Is it possible that sometimes those companions are not imaginary but the little ones' guardian angels?
>
> Whatever mystical experiences children enjoy, they usually fade about the time a child enters second or third grade, and many kids seem to expect it. "They [the angels] go back to heaven when you're seven," one little girl explained matter-of-factly. Some kids mourn the loss, and others barely react. By the time children are nine or ten, most will have completely forgotten

their early mystical experiences, as if a giant eraser had wiped everything away from their memories.[1]

After the child is born and as the years unfold, it is as though veils of forgetfulness descend. The memory of the child's early spiritual experiences gradually fades from the outer mind. The material world, with all of its challenges, becomes the focus of attention and of the continual striving for self-mastery.

This is as it should be. After all, each child has a mission, and he must work to develop the physical and mental faculties and all the elements of outer life that are needed to fulfill that mission. However, the goal is not to entirely leave behind the inner life but to build the outer life in harmony with the inner life; to integrate the two.

If the child's inner life is nurtured in those crucial early years, this integration becomes the guiding principle throughout life. It becomes part of the child's core identity. It is during the first years of life that the child is actively building himself, even when the memories of those early mystical experiences are beginning to fade from the outer mind.

Meeting the changing needs of the child

What a child needs at one period of life may not be what she needs at another stage of life. In fact, what was once helpful may at a later stage be an obstacle. Take for instance, feeding your child. It is essential at the early stages, but as soon as the child is capable of feeding herself, she will push your hand away and demand to do it herself. We have all heard the wail of a young child, "Me do it!" She is asking you to help her to do it all by herself. Self-mastery is her most important goal.

Daniel Pink's New York Times bestselling book, *Drive: The Surprising Truth About What Motivates Us*, assembles research that identifies autonomy, mastery and purpose as the real motivators of human beings. These intrinsic motivations are far more powerful than the old carrot and stick motivators of rewards and punishments for both adults and children.

It is well known that children grow and develop into adults in stages of physical, mental and emotional development. What is not so well known is that spiritual development also takes place in clearly-defined stages.

Before birth

The most rapid stage of a child's development is actually before birth. There are times in those first nine months when brain cells are developing at the astounding rate of millions per minute. Science is informing us that the child is aware before birth. He can see, hear and taste. Many people also have sub-conscious memories of what happened when their mothers were pregnant.

The mother's body is the child's first home. That home is the physical body of the mother, but also the emotions, thoughts, spiritual aspirations and memories of the mother and her environment. The child experiences all of this while yet in the womb. For nine months the child is building a physical body and all that is necessary to live in the outside world.

At the moment of birth, it is as though a flame of life is ignited. The first breath fills the lungs. The child comes into the world with boundless energy and unlimited love for those fortunate enough to be his parents.

The child is ready to develop according to the general plan

for all children and according to the unique plan of his own blend of capabilities and inherent strengths.

Birth to 6 years: the absorbent mind

Within the new environment, rich with sensory experiences —all the sights, sounds, tastes and textures of a new world—the child takes everything in, learning effortlessly and building himself out of what he absorbs.

Maria Montessori coined a wonderful phrase to describe the first six to seven years of life: the absorbent mind. During this time, the child is like a sponge, learning by being immersed in life and taking in everything from the environment without discrimination.

The modern science of neurology is now confirming Montessori's insight into the nature of the child. Ronald Kotulak, 1994 Pulitzer Prize winner for his writing on early brain development, writes:

> The brain is now seen as a super-sponge.... The brain can reorganize itself with particular ease early in life during crucial learning periods. Information flows easily into the brain through "windows" that are open for only a short duration. Then the windows close, and the fundamental architecture of the brain is completed.[2]

The great work of the child during this period is nothing less than to construct himself. He creates himself out of the experiences in his environment. He can construct himself only out of what is available. So we must ask, is he surrounded by love or is he surrounded by discord and harshness? Is he surrounded by objects to touch and handle and gaze upon or is he left alone in a crib in a barren room? Does he hear his language spoken lovingly and at great length, or does he hear voices filled with strident anger or toneless depression? These are the resources the child uses to construct himself, no matter whether they are positive or negative. That is the double-edged sword of the absorbent mind. It does not judge whether something is helpful or harmful. It simply takes it in and builds itself out of it.

If positive factors are absent in the child's early life, development may not be optimal. But researchers like Craig Ramey have discovered that early intervention can be a help. He worked with a group of low income, low-birth-weight infants and their mothers, exposed them to enriched environments, and found that this intervention had lasting positive effects on the children's intellectual and emotional development.[3] Ramey also found that work with the emotional lives of the children was just as important as their physical and mental environment.[4]

Much of what the child learns in his early years is done through the process of absorption from the environment. For example, the child learns a new language simply by the process of absorption. The child hears the language spoken and watches your mouth. He begins to babble, says single words and phrases and then, in just a few short years, he has the mastery of a complete language—or more than one in a multilingual household.

In actual fact, it is much easier for a child to master physical coordination, learn good manners and acquire even complex skills such as reading and writing in the first six years of life than it will be later on. He can do basic math with concrete objects, learn the basics of science and even learn about the parts of speech effortlessly in the absorbent mind. If we wait to teach these things until after the child enters the next stage of life, the reasoning mind, he must study and memorize every-thing. The absorbent phase is a period of rapid growth, of developing the sense of self and of mastering basic skills.

The major sensitive periods of development for the early years of a child's development from birth to 6 are the following:

- Movement: birth to 4 years
- Refinement of the senses: birth to 5 years
- Language: birth to 6 years
- Order: 12 months to 3½ years
- Manners, grace and courtesy: 2 to 6 years
- Writing: 4 to 5 years
- Numbers: 4 to 5½ years
- Reading: 5½ years

In addition to the sensitive periods for general development, Maria Montessori discovered that there are powerful and dynamic spiritual sensitive periods that govern deep impulses for the growth of the inner lives of our children. Children can also absorb in these years positive attitudes, devotion, gracious behavior, a love of beauty and a reverence for life that are the raw materials of a rich spiritual life.

The sensitive periods for spiritual development include the following:

- Love and protection: birth to 6 years
- Religious formation: birth to 6 years

In *The Religious Potential of the Child*, Sofia Cavalletti wrote about observing a child singing to a statue of Jesus. The child continued singing for more than forty minutes. She was not aware that anyone was observing her. There was no other external activity going on. What motivated her other than something deep within, unseen by us but nevertheless present and active? She was surely in the throes of a sensitive period for devotion.

Children watch us and learn from what we do, and they unconsciously form their attitudes and behaviors largely from what they see. We have often heard the old adage, "Do what I say, not what I do!" But we all know it doesn't work that way. We can't fool our children; they see beyond our words.

However, even in this stage, it is important to remember that children also bring with them who they are, and this can enable them to transcend the limitations of their environment, as this story shows. A three-year-old girl did not attend any kind of preschool, had few contacts outside the home and had no one within the home who spoke of spiritual things, as neither parent believed in God. One day she asked her father, "Where does the world come from?"

Her father answered with a well-reasoned, materialistic view. But then he added, "However, there are some who say this all comes from a very powerful being, and they call him God."

The child began joyously running and dancing around the room exclaiming, "I knew what you told me wasn't true; it is Him, it is Him!"[5]

The understanding of the absorbent period and of later stages of development will enable you to provide the appropriate kinds of spiritual stories, lessons and experiences your child will benefit from at each stage. Since the child is always a whole child, physical, mental, emotional and spiritual needs are always in some way united. When all these levels are addressed, the spirit is nourished even as the body and mind are fed.

6 to 12 years: the reasoning mind

After the age of about 6 or 7, children enter into the reasoning mind that they will retain for the rest of their lives. This mind is a wonderful thing, allowing us to ponder and learn, to think abstractly and synthesize information. Among the great focuses of the next six years of life is a powerful interest in facts about the world in which they live.

Children love to learn, especially when they find something that interests them and strikes their imagination. Montessori approaches this period with a view of the universe so that all future studies of the child will have a connection to the whole. Everything from the solar system to the geological eras, biology, and how language and numbers developed is told with a story and followed up with multiple choices of lessons. The essentials of all of the sciences, math and geometry, as well as learning to communicate through reading and writing are established during these years.

The elementary years are the prime time in the child's life for moral formation. Children can easily understand the generosity of the universe and its workings—even the plants give us the oxygen we need to breathe!

Children at this stage of life incessantly ask, "Why?" They are passionate about learning what is right and wrong. This is the time your child will be interested in your personal rules or moral standards and in your religion or spiritual path.

The major sensitive periods for the second six years include:

- Imagination: 6 to 9 years
- Acquiring culture and learning facts: 6 to 12 years
- Moral formation: 6 to 12 years

12 to 18 years: developing the social self

In the next cycle of life, the teenage years, we find the passage of the child in the family to the man or woman in society. The child begins to seek his place in the world and to think abstractly. Interestingly enough, when puberty arrives, the intellect takes a lesser role as changes in the young person's physical body become a focus of attention. Teens become more interested in finding their way in the society of their peers and in sports and activities than in learning.

Areas of development in these years include the following:

- Abstract thinking
- Social sensibility
- Heroism and following role models
- Economic independence

Teens are searching for role models, heroes to emulate, and for ways to play a meaningful part in life. For many, the search focuses on finding friends and activities that uplift rather than tear down their inner life. They seek practical ways to live the values they developed in earlier years and to include their spiritual life in daily life, which can be a challenge when they are not among those who share the same values and inner life.

The teen years are a time for experimentation and we often see teens, even those with the best of intentions, exercising poor judgment. Unfortunately, teens' higher decision-making skills develop more slowly than their physical bodies. The frontal areas of the brain are where emotions and thinking merge. The executive functions of good judgment in this part of the brain reach full development only in the late teens and early twenties.[6]

Perhaps the world of fast cars, plentiful drugs and alcohol, violent and highly sexual media content are not what our young people are wired for. They are not ready for it and are easily overwhelmed by the lure of these many outer attractions. Meditation and mindfulness exercises have many benefits to offer teens, and these have even been documented medically to have both physiological and psychological benefits.[7]

The strength to overcome the temptations of the world is not born in these teen years. It comes from the accumulation of what has transpired in the earlier stages of development. Montessori wrote:

> The more a man's inner life shall have grown nor-
> mally, organizing itself in accordance with the provi-
> dent laws of nature, and forming an individuality, the
> more richly will he be endowed with a strong will and
> a balanced mind.

To be ready for a struggle, it is not necessary to have struggled from one's birth, but it is necessary to be strong. He who is strong is ready.[8]

Once the years of young adulthood arrive, there is new-found interest in reflection, refining goals, and forming lifelong relationships. There is a capacity to enter into the deeper mysteries of spirituality, finally leading to the potential for a full integration with the spiritual self as young people enter their thirties.

Supporting the natural cycles of development

The essential premise of this book is that the potential for a spiritual life is present within every child. It is alive, rich and deep during each of the stages of development, as surely in the spiritual realm as in the stages of physical and intellectual development. Maria Montessori reminds us that the goal of education is not so much the imparting of knowledge as the unveiling and developing of spiritual energy. Such a powerful reminder!

Educators have long understood that the intellectual development of the child can be most effectively fostered by supporting the natural cycles of development. This principle is equally applicable to the child's inner life.

If the child is still in the early stage of developing love and trust, it is not the time to force him to memorize our theology. It is not the time to work on moral formation, which will so easily develop at its proper time. Cavalletti writes:

We must not anticipate or confuse the times. If we do, we preclude the child's access to that aspect of God the child most needs. In our estimation, we compromise the very moral foundation, which should be based on love.[9]

The child's inner life can most effectively be supported if we understand these cycles and work with them. In the next chapters we will take a look at the development of the child more closely, from prenatal to age twelve, with many practical activities for you to engage in with your child at each stage.

3

Life before Birth

Maria Montessori was a pioneer in early childhood education, and when she proposed that children as young as three were capable of learning something, this was a new and controversial idea.

"When do you say the education of children should begin?" a parent once asked Montessori.

"Nine months before they are born!" was her stunning reply.

How do you nurture the inner life of the child who is not yet born? Actually, the best place to begin is before you even conceive.

Conception itself is a great mystery. If conception occurs it is as though, through our voluntary act of sexual union, we are witness to the act of creation. What we can do is prepare to receive the gift.

Physical preparation

We begin by preparing to receive the child into our lives by our physical readiness. It begins with the state of health and of consciousness of the parents before and during conception. Many parents change their diets to nutritious whole foods as soon as they consider getting pregnant, and the earlier they can begin, the better. The health and strength and store of nutrients to support a new life are not built overnight.

If you are a mother preparing to conceive, pure fresh foods, pure water and plenty of sleep are important to help you become as strong and healthy as you can be. Some type of general or specific prenatal vitamin and mineral supplement can also play a vital role, since much of our food is grown in depleted soil and does not have all the nutrition our bodies need. It is especially important to have adequate folic acid to prevent neural tube defects during the first weeks of pregnancy. A doctor or nutritionist can help identify the mother's specific physical needs.

An obvious step to take when considering pregnancy is to stop smoking (associated with asthma and low birth weight of the child) or using recreational drugs of any kind. Talk with your doctor about any prescription or non-prescription medications you are taking to see if they should or could be discontinued.

The use of alcohol by the mother during pregnancy can cause severe damage to the development of the child, and the most serious damage can be done to the fetus in the first few weeks, before many mothers are even aware that they are pregnant.

Fetal alcohol syndrome is not a curable disease; it is a birth defect. Where the damage occurs depends in part on when the drinking takes place.[1] In general, it is the higher functions of the brain that are damaged, those areas that form the vessel for the perception and expression of the child's spiritual life.

There is controversy as to how much alcohol it takes to cause fetal alcohol syndrome. Medical authorities are not in total agreement, so the best course of action is to stop drinking entirely if you are considering pregnancy.

Emotional Preparation

Most of us do not consciously remember events that happened before the age of three or four. Because of that, scientists and psychologists at one time made assumptions that there are no memories or psychologically significant events during this period. It is now well-known that this is not the case and that the events of the earliest years of the child's life have profound effects on later development.

We also want to be ready to receive a child on the emotional level. The motives for conception play a part in our readiness to have a baby and in the newborn baby's sense of wellbeing. Is our motive some kind of self-gratification or proving of oneself or pleasing others, or is it a sincere love and a desire to sponsor life? The motive of the parents sets the psychological climate for the child's entire life.

In the late 1970s Chicago psychologist Helen Wambach did regressions of more than 750 people and reported on her results in the ground-breaking book, *Life Before Life.* Eighty-six percent of these people remembered their life before birth and could recall their mother's feelings and thoughts while they were in the womb.[2]

Wambach's book gives many specific examples of people's pre-birth recollections. Said one person about her mother, "I knew she wanted me to be special and that everything would be right for me.... She felt mildly resigned and somewhat happy and proud. It was more something she had to do and then wanted to do. She did not mind being pregnant, it was okay." Another recalls, "My mother cried a lot and didn't really want me," while a third individual remembers, "I was clearly aware of the emotions of my mother. She was a little sad and upset because of Dad not giving her enough attention, and she was also deeply happy."[3]

These stories remind me of a friend who became pregnant unexpectedly and considered aborting her child. Once she and her husband made the decision to keep the baby, they had a special celebration to tell the unborn child how welcome she was. So remember to welcome the growing life within you. Send love to your child and gratitude for his presence in your life.

Other relationships in the parents' lives also have a profound effect on the development of the child in the womb. Research from the Fels Institute in Yellow Springs, Ohio, showed that there are three psychological factors that have the highest impact on the success of a pregnancy. First is the desire to have the child. Second is the relationship between the parents. Third is the relationship of the woman with her own mother.

Pregnancy and children bring a whole new dimension to the relationship between mother and father. Instead of lovers focused on one another, they are now parents focused on the child, and this change in itself can create stress in the relationship. It is important to be able to talk about these issues and work through them as they arise. Women who want to have children would also find it helpful to work on resolving any difficulties in their relationships with their mothers, since pregnancy tends to bring up both conscious and subconscious memories of how a woman was parented, especially how she was mothered.

Mental preparation

What about our mental preparation and the child's mental development in the womb?

An important question is whether babies learn in the womb. Can a mother's thoughts and actions affect the mental development of her child? Science is finally catching up to Montessori's understanding that learning begins nine months before birth. Overwhelming evidence now demonstrates that the child is conscious, aware and receptive before birth. The child in the womb is an intelligent, conscious individual, seeking relationships, learning language, and searching for love and affection from his parents.

If the child is conscious at birth, he didn't suddenly become conscious in the birth canal. Babies born at seven and even six months are also conscious when they are born. So when does conscious awareness start? Michael Gabriel, psychologist and author of *Voices from the Womb,* says, "My work has convinced me that our awareness begins much further back than psychologists once believed, and that human consciousness extends beyond the limits of the five senses and the brain."[4]

Thomas Verney writes in his book, *The Secret Life of the Unborn Child,* "The unborn child is a feeling, remembering, aware being, and because he is, what happens to him—what happens to all of us—in the nine months between conception and birth molds and shapes personality, drives and ambitions in very important ways."[5]

One way to enhance the child's mental and spiritual development is to listen to inspiring music while the child is in the womb. Women in cultures dating back to ancient China and Greece used music to assist the baby's harmonious development. Music was thought to be an active force in life and the choice of music was considered to be of great import.

The research of such authors as David Tame, Thomas Verney and Don Campbell suggests that babies thrive on classical music. Listening to beautiful music may become a habit after the baby is born, as it did with me. The child with whom I listened to music the most developed her own habit and listens to beautiful classical music as she does her housework and school work.

One of my favorite stories of how the unborn child perceives music comes from the life of Boris Brott, conductor of the Toronto Symphony Orchestra. Brott was given a new score to work on. He said as he read the score the cello line jumped out at him. It was an unfamiliar piece of music so he was a bit surprised. He happened to mention this in a telephone conversation with his mother, a cellist. She began to laugh and told him that this piece was one that she played while she was pregnant with him.

New research shows that a stimulating mental environment for the mother before and during pregnancy is likely to also enhance the neurological development of the child in the womb.[6] Pregnancy is a wonderful time to begin reading books about child development, so that when the child arrives the parents have more of a sense of what to expect month by month and year by year.

Communication is another important way to enrich your child's mental and emotional development before birth. You can communicate with your baby each day both mentally and physically. Fathers also like to rub mommy's belly and talk to the child. Babies are even known to kick back the same number of times a dad pats. Bonding begins before birth, and both parents and child are likely to feel closer after many months of pre-birth communication.[7]

Spiritual preparation

Are the sublime moments of union between man and woman simply experiences of pure pleasure? Or is there something more? What is this magnificent moment of conception itself?

Most of us probably do not consider our sexual nature as a vital part of our spiritual lives. Yet many spiritual traditions consider the sexual act as not only an expression of love but also a sacred moment of exchange of the sacred fire between man and woman, symbolic of the union of the male and female forces of the universe.

With this understanding, some parents enter into a holy state of meditation prior to sexual union. They attune with the divinity of the mother by listening to the "Ave Maria" and with the divinity of the father by listening to "The Lord's Prayer" or other sacred music. Many couples consecrate their union by saying a prayer together, meditating or visualizing light around themselves. We can make every moment of our lives something holy if we make it so in our consciousness.

The period of life before birth is an exciting frontier to explore. There are many unknowns, yet we are certain that the baby is living inside the mother's physical body and inside of her feeling world as well. The mother's spiritual experiences during pregnancy will have an effect on the child, just as her physical, emotional and mental experiences help form the life within her.

Many women find a cleansing of the mind and emotions through some form of prayer or meditation can bring positive effects during pregnancy. One technique is to focus your attention on your heart and visualize a white light burning there. Then see the light expand and radiate out from your heart. Let it bless your baby and your entire family. If you wish you can expand the light to your community, your nation and the entire world and ask for all to be blessed.

Some women enjoy meditating on beautiful images that are sacred to them, whether from religion, art or nature. In ancient Greece, mothers meditated upon beautiful images, statues and music to assist their child's prenatal development. To focus on the beauty of nature or on inspirational objects of art is calming and spiritually uplifting for both mother and the unborn child. Taking regular walks during pregnancy is good for the body and the spirit.

Pregnancy is a wonderful time to read uplifting biographies, which is a kind of meditation on the qualities of soul and spirit that the child can bring to fruition. Another type of meditation focuses on the child's stages of physical development. You can also collect pictures of the child at each week of development, and during that week gaze at the image of a child at that particular stage of development and pray for the development to be safe and complete for your child and every child at this stage.* You may feel like you are actually taking part in God's miraculous creation with this simple meditation, and in fact, you are.

As you meditate on the love in your heart, you might try a meditation suggested by quantum physics that tells us that energy is responsive to thought. In this meditation, you place your left hand over your heart and your right hand over the image on which you are meditating and send your love in a flow of energy from your heart to the image of the child. Sending your love to your unborn child in this way may be more powerful than we will ever know.

Simple prayer is also a wonderful way to send your love to the child. Mother Teresa described prayer with these words: "Our prayers should be burning words coming forth from the furnace of hearts filled with love."[8] Your prayers for your child and for the children of the world can truly make the difference in enabling the child in your womb and all children to find wholeness and to feel welcome in this world.

---

* *A Child is Born,* by Lennart Nillson, is filled with exquisite pictures showing stages of development of the child in the womb. Wonderful images of the child in the womb are also available freely on the Internet. *Conception to Birth,* a video by Alexander Tsiaris, is available on YouTube and at www.ted.com.

4

Falling in Love with God
Birth to 6 Years

One day a five-year-old girl named Linda noticed a beautiful butterfly, and she followed it.

Suddenly she felt a change come over her. Everything seemed to open up around her, she could see more clearly. She felt filled with joy and warmth throughout her whole body.

The experience was strong and clear. Linda burst into tears of joy and ran to her mother saying, "Mommy, I know God!"

I have been teaching young children since 1972, and I am repeatedly and most deeply impressed with the spiritual interests and keen insight that children display. While raising my own three children, their spontaneous awe and gratitude for life has continually inspired me.

Maria Montessori discovered that the youngest child, from birth through age 6, is in the sensitive period for spiritual/ religious formation. The child has the potential during this time to develop an inclination toward the inner life of the spirit. Because of this natural tendency to incline to the inner life of the spirit, it is easy to help your young child develop habits of devotion and of talking with God.

This internal inclination towards the spirit may happen naturally in children even when there are indifferent or unfavorable environmental conditions that do not support spiritual growth. Imagine what more can happen in an environment rich in spiritual content and stimulus that corresponds with what the child is experiencing inwardly.

Montessori had seen profound evidence of the spiritual life of children in her work and she long desired to more deeply pursue the spiritual development of children, but as she entered her eighties she realized that her time was limited and she sought the help of others who could carry on this aspect of her mission. She commissioned one of her co-workers and assistants, Gianna Gobbi, to take up the work of how to teach religious and spiritual development using the principles of her method. Dr. Sofia Cavalletti, an Italian noblewoman and scholar of Hebrew and scripture, became interested in the religious formation of the child and joined Gobbi in the mid-1950s.

Cavalletti and Gobbi accepted the challenge Maria Montessori had placed before them. They both spent the next fifty years of their lives diligently pursuing the path of observing and nurturing the spiritual development of children, working week after week directly with children in Cavalletti's home in Rome.

Gobbi wrote *Listening to God with Children*. Cavalletti documented her work in several books, including *The Religious Potential of the Child*. These women brought to fruition what Montessori said was the true educational mission of her methods, allowing the spiritual nature of the child to reach its full flowering.

I had the opportunity to study with Sofia Cavalletti on several occasions: for a week in Bergamo, Italy, in 1975, again at her home in Rome, and for a month in the United States when Jerome Berryman brought her to Houston in 1978. Her teaching and systematic work was an inspiration to me. Whether one wishes to develop a religious program that works within the context of a church or develop a program to nurture the inner life in a more secular manner, the ground-breaking work of these two women offers foundational principles to build upon.

After nurturing thousands of children in their spiritual formation, Cavalletti concluded that the religious work of the young child can be summed up in the Italian word "innamoramento," which means, simply, "falling in love." The first

Sofia Cavalletti and
Mary Ellen Maunz
June 1978, Houston, Texas

spiritual work of the child is simply to fall in love with God!

From the first days of life, our children fall in love with us and we fall in love with them—every parent experiences this. Our children can also fall in love with God, and this is something we can help them to do. First and foremost we can teach our children that God is love and God loves all of us.

Cavalletti wrote:

> We could perhaps say that, since the religious [spiritual] experience is fundamentally an expression of love, it corresponds in a special way to the child's nature. We believe that the child, more than any other, has need to love because the child himself is rich in love. The child's need to be loved depends not so much

on a lack that requires filling, but on a richness that seeks something that corresponds to it.[1]

Dr. Elisabeth Caspari, my longtime friend and mentor on the Montessori path, was a good friend and colleague of Maria Montessori. She was also a deeply spiritual and devotional woman. She loved God and she loved people. One of her favorite sayings was that she loved to see "God on two feet." In other words, she loved to see people expressing acts of kindness and love for one another.

Love and trust do not develop in a vacuum—they develop in relationships. The first relationship that sets the pattern of the child for life is the relationship with parents.

When your baby cries and you pick her up and soothe her with your tender caress and gentle voice, she experiences love in a very tangible way. She also learns to trust that you will be there when she needs you.

The primary period for the development of trust is birth to 18 months. If that foundation of receiving love and learning to trust others is not laid down in those early months, it becomes difficult for the child to trust in later years. Robin Karr-Morse and Meredith S. Wiley, in their remarkable book *Ghosts from the Nursery: Tracing the Roots of Violence,* outline scientific studies looking back to the early lives of violent criminals, which reveal an overwhelming pattern of neglect and abuse in the first two years of life. When a baby is neglected and cries in protest, and then is spanked for crying, the neurological connections for self-calming are never developed. Rage develops without self-control, and individuals may lash out at any provocation, real or imagined.

As the child's nervous system is developing, the calmer and

more responsive we are, the more we will help her develop the neural circuits of responsiveness and the ability to self-calm. Attachment research has shown that when we respond to the smiles and coos of our child, she learns to respond back to us. Children who have depressed and unresponsive caregivers do not learn the same ability.

A smiling face that brings tender concern rather than harshness or anger may become the key influence for the child to be able to feel safe and at home in the universe. One might say that mother and father represent God to their newborn children. The child knows what to expect from life by what he experiences through us. Can we be the gentle filter through which the child experiences the love of God?

I read somewhere that no child has ever been loved as much as he or she wished. But we can love with all we've got and make certain our children feel safe and secure. And if we want to help our child fall in love with God, we can start by creating an environment that is full of love and appreciation for the wonders of this beautiful world.

Harmony in the home

In these very early stages of life, perhaps the most important thing you can do to nurture your child's spirituality is to maintain harmony in the home.

With the process of the absorbent mind, the child builds himself using the nourishment he finds in the environment. If we surround him with love and harmony, he will absorb it and build himself from that. If we surround him with arguments and discord, he will build himself from that as well. When we understand this, we may find that our responsibility in raising a child is perhaps greater than we had at first considered, and building a habit of keeping our harmony may be one of the toughest challenges of all. It requires a deep striving for harmony in one's life as well as a generous willingness to surrender one's wishes and make compromises.

Some of us are fortunate to find a life partner with whom we have great harmony. For many, marriage is more like what a friend called "sandpapering." We find the glorious opportunity to work on our rough edges!

Marriage and receiving a child require great adjustments and frequent compromises. Do we have the self-control to sustain harmony when things get tough? When the baby is crying at 3 a.m.? Do we love enough to keep silent when angry words would simply add fuel to the fire?

German lyric poet Rainer Maria Rilke wrote, "For one human being to love another: this is perhaps the most difficult of our tasks, the ultimate, the last test and proof, the work for which all other work is but preparation."[2]

Creating harmony and peace for ourselves and the ones we love is an important step in building a more spiritual way of life. Our own loving and harmonious presence is the most significant force in the life of the child.

Harmony is not only a lack of arguments and discord but a state of being. We can help create it by the way we arrange our day so there is enough time to get ready for work rather than having to rush to be on time. It can be the gentle word of encouragement to our spouse facing a tough decision at work, or a quick phone call to a friend you have not heard from for a while. It can be the smile or a loving touch that makes the day better for those around you.

Beauty and spirituality

There is a deep connection between beauty and spirituality. Stop and think about how we prepare lovely nurseries for our babies using soft, pastel colors. We sing to them. We coo to them, we smile silly smiles and chatter on in that high-pitched tone of voice that mothers and fathers use the world over. We play with them. We *know* what they need. It is simply a shift in gears to think about this in terms of nurturing the inner life.

Take the time to share things of beauty with your children. Whether it is a tiny blossom that is perfectly formed, a seashell on the beach or a grand exhibit at your local art museum, expose your children to beauty and help them to see that life is beautiful. The wide exposure to new things you provide builds patterns of beauty, expands their world view and offers great opportunity for new vocabulary.

Color is based on frequencies of light. People have their definite preferences for color and various colors have long been associated with differing emotions. In creating a spiritual environment that is conducive to the inner life, light pastels work particularly well. Those of us who work with young children have found that some highly sensitive children are over-stimulated by too much red and orange. Pink and yellow are associated with joy and wisdom, while the cool colors of blues and greens are calming and healing. Violet is a favorite for many children.

You might consider using some aspects of Montessori class-rooms the world around, which usually utilize neutral woods, white paint or soft pastels for shelving for all the working materials. These colors make the materials stand out but do not visually distract the child's attention. The materials themselves are colorful and attractive to the child's eye, in a wide variety of clear, simple hues.

Another component of beauty is geometry and harmony of form. Surround your child with inspiring art, pictures of the beauties of nature, the harmonious sound of good music and loving voices. We can all come up a step higher and try to act as a filter for the discord of the world and keep our homes places that remind our children of heaven. Beauty can even be the ten minutes you spend cleaning up the living room or the kitchen at a certain time each day to make your home a little more cheerful and beautiful.

There will be plenty of time in later years for your child to learn about the ugliness, the harshness and suffering in so many parts of the world. When your child has a strong foundation in the beauty and harmony of the inner life, she will be better prepared to deal with those challenges when that time comes.

The importance of beauty was brought home to me while I was working in a charter school in a low income area of a large city in the United States some years ago. Every day on the way to work I went by fields full of cast-off junk, abandoned buildings and homes in disrepair.

As I began to work with the children at the school in September, I found that they were very far behind the academic development of the children I had been working with in other schools. When I thought about why this might be, I felt that seeing only the depressed neighborhood in which they lived, day after day, was one of the blocks to their development. I was reminded of that fateful morning in 1978, in a downtrodden area of New York City, when I first began to comprehend the power of beauty in the life of a child.

One of the first things that I did was to brighten up the

classroom and bring in beautiful plants, crystals and framed pictures. I took the children on field trips to beautiful gardens in the city, museums and lovely parks. We went to beautifully designed offices and met with many different professionals, from architects to veterinarians.

I brought in books to show them—beautiful art, flowers, jewels and architecture. We listened to beautiful music. I read uplifting stories, very different from the depressing stories they regularly heard of the drug and gang violence that plagued the area and impacted the lives of so many of the children in that classroom.

Many of these children came from loving homes, yet many told me about a parent or older sibling in jail. I wanted to give them a sense that there was more to life than what they could see around them. I believed that beauty would bring them a sense of wholeness and put them in touch with a part of themselves that had not yet been awakened.

At the beginning of the school year, I asked the children to draw pictures of what they would do when they grew up. Out of thirty children, only one saw himself as a professional of any kind. Some saw themselves working at Wal-Mart, some as beauticians and garbage truck drivers. I absolutely believe that all work is noble, but I also realized that they did not have a vision of possibilities based on their own potentials. One boy actually saw himself dead on the street. The drawings had almost no color.

In the springtime, I asked the children once again to draw themselves as adults. After one year of beauty, the differences were striking. There had been a gradual flowering of beauty within them, and now more than half had an entirely new vision of what they could be and do. The colors they used were bold and lovely.

One of the most interesting things I observed that year was that in April they were able to organize themselves to independently play a constructive game on the playground. This was something they had not been able to do up to that time. They were so proud of themselves and it was beautiful to my eyes. They had somehow internalized patterns of harmony and order that allowed this spontaneous activity to come forth.

The power of music

Harmony in music is nourishing to the soul. It is also powerful. According to David Tame, author of *The Secret Power of Music,*

> There is scarcely a single function of the body which cannot be affected by musical tones. The roots of the auditory nerves are more widely distributed and possess more extensive connections than those of any other nerves in the body. Investigation has shown that music affects digestion, internal secretions, circulation, nutrition and respiration. Even the neural networks of the brain have been found to be sensitive to harmonic principles.[3]

I personally learned the powerful effects of music a long time ago, when I started systematically working with Beethoven's Nine Symphonies. I was in my early twenties, I was really into music, and began to experiment on myself as to how these pieces of music would affect me. I listened to at least two of the symphonies every day for nearly a full year.

I began to see that the music had specific influences on me. Before too long, I knew which one to use for various situations in my life. If I was sick, I would play the Sixth Symphony and lie under the eucalyptus trees in my backyard. If I was sad, I would play the Seventh Symphony. If I needed to calm down, the Second Symphony worked. As I saw clearly the effects of music in my life, I became more discriminating as to the other music I listened to, and I began to be more conscious of music in my environment in general.

Music is everywhere around us and we often tune it out. Yet it has been known for thousands of years that music has tremendous power to shape our thoughts and even the world in which we live. Confucius said:

> Harmony has the power to draw heaven downwards towards the earth. It inspires men to love the good and to do their duty. If one should desire to know whether a kingdom is well governed, if its morals are good or bad, the quality of its music will furnish forth the answers.[4]

That is an astounding, thought-provoking premise. How does music affect us physically, emotionally and spiritually?

An interesting experiment was done comparing the effects of the music of Bach with that of a heavy metal rock band. Rats were placed into two identical, adjoining cages, complete with food, water and toys. They could freely move from cage to cage. The only difference was the type of music: one cage had Bach, the other heavy metal.

All of the rats stayed, all the time, in the Bach cage. The experimenter, wondering if the phenomenon had something to do with geography, switched the location of the cages. The rats again moved to the cage with Bach.

A researcher named Dorothy Retallack, author of *The Sounds of Music and Plants,* conducted controlled experiments with plants. Her results showed that flowers and vegetables exposed to various forms of rock music experienced stunted and erratic growth and most died. The plants exposed to Western classical and North Indian classical music were healthy and actually grew toward the speakers.[5]

Among the most significant pieces of research about the effects of music comes from India. Dr. T. C. Singh, head of the Department of Botany at Annamalai University in India discovered that classical music causes plants to grow twice as fast as plants without exposure to classical music. He discovered that sound waves increase the movement of protoplasm within cells. Violins with a high-pitched range of sound produce the most movement in protoplasm.[6]

Dr. Singh also discovered that the seeds produced by plants exposed to classical music produced new generations of plants with accelerated growth. This shows us that music can somehow alter the expression of genetic traits in plants. We do not yet know precisely how it may be affecting our children and ourselves, but common sense leads to the conclusion that we are affected as well.

In the field of animal research, physicist Dr. Harvey Bird has made a significant contribution. In conjunction with neurobiologist Dr. Gervasia Schreckenberg, they subjected one group of mice to voodoo drum beats, one group to Strauss waltzes and one group to silence. The drums and waltzes were kept at identical, low volume so the loudness of the sound itself would not affect behavior.

Periodically the mice were tested on their ability to run a maze. The "waltz mice" did slightly better than the "silence mice," while the "voodoo mice" became disoriented and lost ability to run the mazes, even to get food. They were given a three-week reprieve from the music and after the three weeks, the mice subjected to the intense drum beat still could not run the maze successfully.

The mice brains were ultimately dissected, revealing that the mice that heard the voodoo drum beat had abnormal levels of messenger RNA present and neurons were growing in the wrong area. According to Dr. Schreckenberg, "There were no more connections (among the neurons), just wild growth of the neurons." She went on to say, "Everything in life goes in a rhythm, even the life of a single cell. All the biochemical reactions are rhythmic. If that harmony is disrupted by some kind of disharmony, then it can cause detrimental effects."[7]

We may have personal preferences for music that are distinctly not classical. However that may be, the evidence is convincing that classical music of both the West and the East is especially soothing and conducive to a spiritual life. Choose your favorites and play them in your home. Be mindful and observe the effects of different pieces of music on yourself and your children.

If you are not familiar with classical music, try the big three: Beethoven, Bach and Mozart. Mozart in particular has been found to be helpful for children with ADD, showing improvement in focus, mood control, decrease in impulsivity and improved social skills.[8] Many libraries have CDs you can borrow to determine what music you like well enough to purchase. iTunes and other online music sellers allow you to hear a sample before you purchase.

I often like to have music in the background some of the time in my classroom. Classical and Celtic are many children's favorites. Go into any good music store and look under the category of relaxing music to find some good selections that contribute to your physiological and psychological sense of well-being. Some people find music soothing as they work, while others do not like music in the background while they work, so make sure it is not an irritant to your child before you play it as background.

Also remember that periods of quiet and stillness actually contribute to a child's learning. Make music a conscious choice rather than a constant background in your life and the life of your child.

The innocence of the child

Children come into this world with veils of innocence. The word innocence sounds to me like "inner sense"—the sense of the inner life their souls have always known. This innocence is a vital part of their innate spirituality. We protect their bodies with all our might against kidnappers and rapists, against drugs and alcohol. But do we protect their minds and hearts with as much energy? Do we even stop to think that the sounds and images of the media might be among the culprits that rob our children of innocence?

Our children deserve the chance to grow with their innocence intact, especially in these early years. Parents are the ones who can and must act on their behalf by setting standards of what we allow and what we do not allow into our homes.

Television and the media are among the biggest threats to the natural innocence of children. Monsters, superheroes, bad girls and violent cartoons are much of the diet that television provides for children. Movies for children often have adult themes and even questionable language.

I love to watch a good television show as much as anyone, but when my children were little, we got rid of the television set that was in our house. As the children grew older, we got another one, but at that time we were living in a rural environment with no broadcast television, and all we could watch were videos that I chose very carefully.

We all have our tastes and we all have our differing standards, but there are objective facts we can look at. Psychology has identified archetypal images of death and violence that evoke fear in our subconscious minds. When we are continually assaulted by images of violence, sensuality and horror in the media, we as adults have become hardened by them and often find them enjoyable. But what effect are they having on our children?

I find myself cringing at some of the frightening images in television ads, and wondering how young children deal with them. How do they process the images of vampires and werewolves? All these images are taken in by the absorbent mind of the young child and stored in the subconscious. Perhaps in the rush of modern culture we have lost some of our discernment of what is nurturing and what is destructive to the innocence of a child.

I recently watched a show called *Toddlers and Tiaras*. It is about the beauty pageant circuit for babies in arms up to twelve-year-olds. I was shocked to see a three-year-old who had been trained to come on stage and remove some of her garments in a suggestive, strip-tease manner; a seven-year-old writhing and crying in her mother's lap while she had her eyebrows plucked; four- and six-year-olds talking about kicking butt in the pageant and being encouraged by ambitious mothers to crush their opponents.

The contrast between nurturing the child's inner life and desecrating it through focus on inappropriate external values was painfully clear. It reminded me that parents hold tremendous power over their children's lives.

If we want to give our children something better than the mass media provides, that is more uplifting to their spirits, we will have to make some sacrifices. We may have to spend some time to find constructive and beautiful toys, movies and books for our children. We have plenty of choices, so we can be careful shoppers.

Even for babies and toddlers, we can find toys that encourage movement, that are beautiful to the eye and that give the mind and hands something interesting and engaging to do. We can expose them to the beauties of art and nature. We can provide a home that is peaceful and harmonious.

The geometry of perfection

Giving our children the opportunity to gaze upon perfection is to give them a connection to their inner spirituality.

Geometry is everywhere in our world, and pure geometric shapes are important playthings for children. A staple of Montessori classrooms around the world is a set of geometric solids for children to touch, manipulate and name along with two-dimensional geometric shapes for them to trace. You do not need Montessori materials to make these essential shapes available for your child. These materials are simply examples of what you can provide.

Geometric solids for children to handle and name

Perfect two-dimensional forms for children to trace

As children work with these materials, they internalize them as concepts, which Maria Montessori called "keys to the universe." For example, the child can look at a dinner plate or a tire on her tricycle and exclaim with delight, "It's a circle!"

Elisabeth Caspari told a wonderful story that illustrates how deeply children absorb the shapes and sizes they touch. A little girl who had been tracing a set of insets of graduated rectangles was walking to school with her daddy, who was a mechanical engineer. They stopped to watch some workmen at a construction site.

One of the men was preparing to install a window. The little girl looked critically at the window and the opening and said, "Daddy, the window is too small." Her father scoffed and told her that the men carefully measure their windows and openings before they install them. The little girl insisted. So they decided to watch and see what happened. Sure enough, the window was too small.

Consider how frequently the shapes of circle, square and triangle occur in our lives, and then consider how they relate to higher concepts in the conscious and subconscious mind. We hear songs and poems of the circle of life, we speak about the cycles of the seasons. Even time is measured as progression around a circle. Then we see the magnificent image of our Earth from space—the great sphere that is our home.

The square is essential in building. A square is a carpenter's tool to assure that his construction is true. When we speak of an arrangement that is just, we call it "fair and square." When we combine the square and the triangle, we form a pyramid, great symbol of eternity and immortality.

These examples of harmony in form build patterns of harmony in the subconscious and form within the growing mind of the child an inner understanding of the building blocks of life.

Holy places

Sound and form are powerful tools for creating a spiritual atmosphere. Think of the medieval cathedrals of Europe, with their soaring arches drawing the gaze up towards the heavens, the blaze of light and color shining through stained-glass windows, images of saints and angels all around.

Virtually every world religion has its sacred music and its sacred architecture. Churches, synagogues, mosques and temples use color, form and light to create a spiritualized atmosphere. Both the interior and the exterior are designed to provide a prepared environment to lead the soul naturally to a higher awareness. These pages show a few photographs of sacred buildings that I have had the opportunity to visit.

These spiritual environments are conducive to creating a sense of awe and the peace of internal contemplation. I remember being in awe as I entered each of these places, knowing of

Exterior and interior of the Cathedral of the Resurrection, Saint Petersburg, Russia

Left and below:
Exterior and
interior of
Buddhist temples
in South Korea

Above and right:
Interior and
exterior views of
the Blue Mosque,
Istanbul, Turkey

the devotions of thousands of people that had been given in each place. I remember also the quietness that came over me as a child when I went to church with my family.

Take your child to visit holy places in your city or town and when you travel. They don't need to be grand or magnificent structures such as these: many small shrines and neighborhood churches have a beauty and holiness that uplifts the soul.

Invitation to prayer

In the late 1980s I arranged a field trip for my class of elementary children and many of their parents to go to Mexico City for a week. Along with many other fabulous sights such as the pyramids of Teotihuacan and the Museum of Anthropology, we took the children to visit the Shrine of Our Lady of Guadalupe, a beautiful basilica dedicated to Mary, the mother of Jesus.

In the 1500s Mary appeared to a young peasant by the name of Juan Diego. According to the legend, there is an imprint of her image that miraculously appeared on his work apron, his *tilma,* as she was speaking with him. The tilma is on display in the basilica, and scientists who have studied it cannot determine any means by which the image could have been placed on the fabric.

I was very moved to see the love poured out by pilgrims at the shrine, and when we climbed the hillside above the basilica to visit a small chapel there, I knelt to say a prayer. One of my students, about seven years of age, asked me what I was doing. I told her I was saying a prayer. She asked what a prayer was and if I would teach her how she could pray. Fortunately, her mother was present and I asked her if it would be okay. She said she was open to the child being exposed to whatever I might say. I told her very simply that a prayer was a way I would talk to God and tell him how grateful I was for this beautiful place and for the fact that we could come to visit it. I have no idea how that seed of experience may have germinated in this child's inner life, but I was touched that she wanted to know how to pray. Children can be keenly receptive to spiritual and religious activities and want to be involved in your inner life, as I saw that day.

To nurture the inner life of your child, it is helpful for him to see you engaged in spiritual practices that support your own inner life. Invite your child to join you when you meditate or pray. I will give more specifics about prayer for children in chapter 6.

5

Nurturing Spirituality

That only which we have within, can we see without. If we meet no gods it is because we harbor none.

—Ralph Waldo Emerson

Nurturing the inner life of our children is not all beauty and spirit. It is also the day-to-day raising of children who may have behavior issues, learning problems or physical ailments of diverse kinds. Much of what is required to deal with these challenges is simply common sense—what Elisabeth Caspari often called the most *un*common sense. We might call it practical spirituality.

It involves making sure your child eats well, gets enough sleep and has a balance of activity and quiet times and plenty of time with you. It is taking action to provide what your child needs in the way of affection, education and discipline.

After having raised three of my own children and taught dozens of different classes of children, I soon learned that what works for one child does not necessarily work for another. One child may respond to a soft gentle tap when he is out of alignment with his inner spirit. Another needs a powerful voice that is more demanding. We learn to be good parents all over again with each individual child.

Children need to learn what is right and what is wrong. They need to learn what foods are good for them and what foods are not good for them. They need to learn how to be polite and how to ask for help when they need it. They need reassurance that they are loved and that we believe they can do anything they set their minds to. But if a child is hitting her little brother, it is not the best time to tell her how beautiful she is. She needs to stop and think about a better way to handle her anger.

Handling anger

We need to observe what makes our children angry or upset, since those emotions replace the harmony and peace in which their inner life thrives. Lack of sleep, unexpected change or a feeling of powerlessness can make a child upset.

We all get angry at situations or people from time to time—even those we love. Our children are no different. While some believe it is important to vent now and then, tirades of anger can easily become habitual and destructive.

Isaac Luria, Jewish mystic of the fourteenth century, wrote that while other sins harm the "limbs" of the soul, anger harms the whole soul.[1] When people engage in tirades of anger, they expend huge amounts of energy; they are left empty and often still angry while the problem remains unresolved. The relationship with the person on the receiving end of such a tirade could be irreparably harmed. In many cases, when we are angry, we are really angry at ourselves. We project it outward at someone else, thus not resolving the original problem at all.

Should we teach our children to control their anger? I answer this question as an educator, as a parent and as a human being with an unqualified *yes*. We may need to work with ourselves first, then demonstrate how, when something goes wrong, we can chuckle at it rather than say something nasty or unkind —or at least remain calm. It is not helpful to suppress anger, but we can freely discuss how angry or hurt a situation made us feel, and then decide what we may need to do about it or that we will let it go and move on.

Elisabeth Caspari used to tell me that when things went radically wrong and she started getting really upset, her husband would mildly say, "It's the hazards of the navigation, dear." I think of this often when I am nearing the end of my rope—the difficult things that happen are just the hazards of navigating my life.

When your child becomes upset or angry, what do you do? To start with, make sure no one gets hurt—first the children, then yourself. I have been kicked so hard in the shins by a student that I could hardly walk. When children are hysterical or out of control it is better to try to soothe them and talk them down first. What you decide to do about the outburst in the way of correction or discipline needs to come later when they can understand what you are saying to them.

On those rare occasions when you have to physically restrain a child in order to protect him from himself or to protect other children, do so as gently as possible. In the case of a child who is kicking, if you pick him up from behind rather than from the front, you are safer.

The next issue is how to control anger.

I observed a situation one evening in a crowded restaurant in Disney World. A father was sitting at a table in the middle of the room with his daughter, who was probably around three years old. She started to whine, "I want to sit by the window." She kept it up, getting louder and louder by the moment.

The father tried to talk to her at first; when this did not work, he decided to ignore her. She continued to get louder, screaming at her father that she wanted to be by the window, while the other patrons became more and more disturbed.

Several restaurant patrons got up and offered their window

tables to the father and his sobbing child. But by this time the little girl was so worked up that she was under the table, screaming at the top of her lungs, shouting, "No!" She didn't want the table by the window any longer. She was red in the face, getting hoarse and sweating profusely. She was out of control and needed help.

The father made no further attempts to stop his child from screaming. He sat there and finished his meal while the rest of us were ready to tear our hair out. Finally he got up to leave. He picked her up and slung her over his shoulder. She was still screaming.

The most amazing part of the entire scenario is that a woman and an older child got up from the next table, and they all left together, the older child calling the man "Daddy." They were clearly a family. Yet neither her father nor her mother had tried to intervene or give the child any tools whatsoever to control herself. I had no idea what had gone on earlier that day or how she had behaved in other situations, but this child had needed help and neither of her parents seemed to know how to give it to her.

The very next day I was at Orlando airport, waiting to return home. A family with three daughters was ahead of me in the line to check in. The youngest began to whine, "I want to sit by the window!" I couldn't believe what I was hearing. "Oh no," I thought, "is this nightmare going to start all over again with another out-of-control child?"

This time I was pleasantly surprised. The child's mother looked straight at her and firmly but calmly told her to stop whining. She was not going to get a window seat on this flight, but she would have one on the trip home. The child sniffed a few times and the mother had to explain again precisely how the family rotation of window seats was going to work, but she accepted it and that was the end of it. I complimented the mother on her parenting skills when we got onto the plane!

When things get out of control we have to intervene, and there are many constructive ways to do this. The father in Orlando could have told his daughter from the beginning that even though she wanted a window table, there were none available. When she continued to whine he could have firmly told her that was enough and that next time they went to a restaurant they would try to find a table by the window.

If she continued, which many children do, especially at a highly stimulating place like Disney World, he might have told her they would leave the room until she could settle down. If this did not work, he would have to follow up his words with actions and actually leave until his daughter could get control of herself. He might have had to take her back to their hotel and order take-out. Sometimes we need to surrender our adult needs for the sake of our children.

The father and child were possibly playing out a pattern of learned behavior where the child was allowed to vent until she got her way. But it is possible also that the little girl was in the throes of a meltdown from sheer tiredness after a long day, and the father was not accustomed to dealing with such a scene. One single painful evening does not tell the entire story. I felt as bad for the father as I did for the child.

To comfort the inner self, we can teach children that we understand how they feel, but it is possible to let go of the anger without hitting or kicking or screaming. We teach children to "use their words" when they are toddlers and preschoolers, so that rather than kicking or biting they tell other children they do not want them to take their toys or get so close to them.

We may need to hold them, speak soothingly and perhaps give them a special toy they like to hold that helps them calm down. Above all, what we do not want to do is get angry at their anger. It helps to remember that our children will do what we do, not what we say. If your response to a child's anger is your own anger, that is what she learns; even if she gets punished for it while you get off scot free. As children get older we can teach them that it is possible to count to ten, or go to a "peace table" or somewhere neutral to talk things over or calm down.

We have to teach our children that it is not okay to go totally out of control. It is not okay to scream endlessly, to incessantly beg or demand attention, to kick or hit or bite. Ultimately we want to give them tools that will work for self-control, so that even when we are not with them, they have the inner resources to calm themselves down.

We have probably all experienced the profound regret of saying something we wish we had not said. Our children will be grateful and our lives will be calmer if we can find ways to help them avoid the trap of speaking from the place of anger. No matter how difficult it is, teaching our children to attune with their hearts and to live and love in harmony with their deepest natures is among the most important things we can do.

The power of harmony and order

The young child's internal need for order is profound. If you tell your child a favorite story one night, she will likely ask for the same story the next night and the next and the next. If you change something about it, your child will bring it to your attention. There is a security born of what Montessori calls "peaceful sameness." Children like and need order until the internal construction that requires it is over. Then the child is no longer so concerned that things be always the same.

Harmony and order are important for the health of the soul. Order in itself helps to produce harmony. Maria Montessori identified the sense of order as one of the universal characteristics of the young child. We have often heard it said that "order is heaven's first law." This principle is especially powerful in the first years of life, up to about age six.

One day, Elisabeth Caspari overheard a conversation between a mother and Montessori that illustrates the importance of establishing habits of order in the early years. The mother asked Montessori for help with her daughter, who never cleaned up after herself. Montessori politely asked the mother how old her daughter was. The mother replied, "Seventeen." Montessori smiled and said, "Madame, you are about fourteen years too late!"

Although children do establish patterns in their early years, we also say that "where there's life there's hope!" Our children can and do change and it is never too late to help them develop their best qualities, even though it may take more conscious effort later in life.

An important insight comes from understanding that children's sense of order develops approximately from eight months to three years of age. They can whine, cry and act out of sorts when something in the environment is out of place. Montessori tells a story illustrating this in *The Secret of Childhood*.

She saw a mother and her child of about three years of age in a park. The weather began to warm up and the mother took off her coat and placed it over her shoulder. The child began to whine for seemingly no reason. She got increasingly agitated and kept crying out, "Coat, shoulder!" The mother was mystified and kept trying to calm her child. As the child escalated her fussiness, the mother was obviously frustrated.

Observers in the park may have judgmentally thought about how naughty the child was. Montessori watched and realized that the child was out of sorts because a coat does not belong on the shoulder! She went up to the mother and quietly offered to help her put her coat on. The mother was rather astonished but did as this strange woman suggested. Immediately the child calmed down.[2]

Again, we come back to meeting the needs of the inner spirit. We can meet them far more effectively when we know what they are and recognize them when they arise. In situations such as this one with the mother and her coat, we do not understand, because we no longer remember the powerful forces of internal development we experienced as young children.

In a Montessori school, we set up the classroom the way we want it at the beginning of the school year and do our best to leave it that way all year, or at least until after a vacation. This gives the children the ability to find what they want out of many choices and put lessons back when they are finished.

You might be laughing out loud right now, saying, "Yeah, right—my child putting things away!" However, what we see in a Montessori classroom is that amazingly, the children quickly —and for the most part, effortlessly—do learn to put all their work away, leaving it ready for the next child. They do this each and every day.

I have had many parents come to school and observe their children behaving in class in a way they have never seen at home. Perhaps the expectation is clearer in class, and it is "just the way we do it here." But children can also learn to do this at home. We do not have to be rigid and demanding, but we can let our children know that when they take their toys out, they are expected to put them back again. We have to model the same thing with our own belongings in the home.

I learned most clearly how important this order is with my own children when they were young. We moved several times and each time, the youngest ones would feel very uncomfortable until we fixed up their rooms with all their familiar things. I made this my first priority and the rest of the house could wait. (My own first priority would have been my kitchen, but with children we do learn selflessness!)

You can provide a rhythm for your child's life with a basic routine. This routine might include consistent times for meals, baths, cycles of rest and cycles of activity. You do not have to always do the same things at the same times every day, but a basic order to daily events is vitally important for your child to be able to develop a sense of security about life.

The power of example

Above all else, the essential message for the child's spiritual development is that there is love in the universe, and that great love can be found both within and without. Of all the things we can have and become in this life, the most important is learning to be loving and kind. The Apostle John wrote: "This is the message that you have heard from the beginning, that you should love one another.... God is love; and he that dwelleth in love dwelleth in God, and God in him."[3]

This is not only a Christian message. The Dalai Lama wrote, "If you want others to be happy, practice compassion. If you want to be happy, practice compassion."[4]

The Buddha himself was asked by a disciple. "Would it be true to say that a part of our training is for the development of love and compassion?" The Buddha answered, "No it would not be true to say this. It would be true to say that the whole of our training is for the development of love and compassion."[5]

Rumi, great thirteenth-century poet of the Islamic world, once wrote a poem about Moses meeting a shepherd who was talking to God, offering to do anything for him. Moses tried to intervene, believing that the man was too familiar with God. God rebuked Moses for separating him from the shepherd and said that the ways of worship are not as important as the quality of the heart. "I don't hear the words," God said, "I look inside."[6] It is all about love.

Children have their own unique approach to spirituality. We can help them develop a way of life that will lead to inner harmony and a deep connection to spirit. It is not helpful to give children metaphysical words and concepts they cannot understand. Instead, we can teach children to love life by instructing them at their own level, with vocabulary they can understand and with situations relating to their life experiences.

Elizabeth Caspari tells of a time when Montessori was asked by a young mother, "How do I teach religion to my child?" Caspari marveled at Montessori's answer: "You don't teach religion to your child, you live it before him!" Our actions speak louder than words. Our real commitments and daily lifestyle choices are what count even more than our teaching moments and lessons.

It is the things our children see us do that they will absorb and become. Compassion and empathy are learned. Even two-year-olds want to help a crying friend. Visualize yourself in the grocery store. You are hurrying along with your toddler seated

in the grocery cart. You hear a child crying the next aisle over. Your child cocks her head and listens. Then she looks at you. What do you do?

If you ignore the crying, your child will learn to ignore calls of distress. Or do you comment that it sounds like someone is crying, then suggest you go take a peek to make sure the little child is not alone and afraid?

A good motto to live by is, "A child is watching you." Living a life of kindness, service and ethics is a gift you can give to your child that will hold her in good stead through all of life. Teach your child to love by loving. Awaken your child's compassion by responding to the pain of others and by serving whenever possible.

It is important to teach your child about your spiritual path. This is especially so beginning at age six or seven when the child enters into the development of his reasoning mind and of moral awareness. But in the rich first years of the absorbent mind, even before that stage of the reasoning mind, we can demonstrate our love and faith in our daily lives so that the child absorbs spirituality as a way of life.

The power of supporting your child's strengths

It is so important to bring out the spirit of the child, to see inwardly with your inner sight the loving, good behavior of the child. Before it even manifests, you just have to know it is there.

Many parents do a great job supporting their children, but some do not. Unfortunately we see that many parents do the opposite—they are often critical and sometimes even judgmental of their children. They criticize them when they make mistakes while ignoring good behavior. They speak harshly to them or say nasty things right in front of them. Perhaps the parents were treated that way themselves. Perhaps their boss yelled at them. Perhaps the parents' own inner critic gets the best of them.

I recommend the movie *Like Stars on Earth* as one of the best that has ever been made about a teacher and the power of vision. It is a deeply moving story of a boy with dyslexia who is doing very poorly in school. He is criticized and ridiculed by his parents, teachers and other students. When he is sent to a new school, one of the teachers notices that he has great artistic ability, and he starts to focus on the child's strengths instead of criticizing his weaknesses. The boy makes astounding progress. He is literally transformed by the vision his caring teacher holds for him and what he can accomplish.

This film touches my heart so deeply because of the children I have taught who came to school with their confidence already in tatters because they had not learned to read, write or compute as quickly as their peers, or because their parents were somehow disappointed in them. Having a learning disability or developing at a slower pace is far more than an academic problem; it affects the child's entire being and self-image.

We can always find something each child is good at, that he can make progress in and then gradually get him involved in the path of learning, no matter how rapid or slow the progress might be. Clearly not every child is a genius, yet every child *has* genius—some area of life in which they can excel. Helping them find this competence is helping them get in touch with the power of their own unique spirit.

Sometimes the problem is as simple as the fact that the child was never properly taught. Sometimes it is much more complex than that. Finding the cause and core of a learning difficulty can be difficult and time consuming. As parents and teachers we may have to dig deep within ourselves to find the skill and patience to help a child with learning disabilities.

The power of the ability to see the child's strengths is the power to bring them to fruition. Support for your child's strengths and focusing on the good can be a tremendously powerful force in your child's life.

The power of gratitude

Gratitude is a powerful way to help your child learn to see the positives in life rather than dwell on the limitations, which come to all of us at one time or another. It is not the limitations that matter; but the attitude we take toward them.

In my own childhood and in the childhood of my own children, the book *The Little Engine That Could,* by Watty Piper, was like a family friend. We read the book again and again. Do you remember the key phrase in the book? "I think I can, I think I can, I think I can." And he did! I always tried to raise my own children with the "can-do spirit," and this book was a lovely aid to that message.

An amazing true life story of someone who has lived with gratitude is Andrea Bocelli, the blind singer. He has been blind since the age of twelve. Many of us have heard him sing, but few know that before he began singing he went to law school and practiced as a defense attorney for a year. He is the father of three children. He rides bikes and horses and has even trained horses. Andrea, according to his mother, "lives in the same manner in which he sings, with an open heart."[7] He is a man who demonstrates gratitude for what he has rather than what he does not have.

You can encourage the sense of gratitude in your children by being grateful yourself. If you see a beautiful day dawning, say, "Thank you, universe, for this beautiful day." If you see something good, no matter how simple it may seem—a lovely flower, a tall strong tree, a beautiful butterfly—draw your child's attention to it and give thanks for it. Talk to your children about the wonders of the earth and all of creation, which never cease to amaze us with their beauty. Be grateful for kindnesses and loving friends in your life.

Children don't artificially segment their lives into a spiritual world and a material world. All of life is one whole to the child. The power of gratitude will change your children's lives, even as you, the parent, will be changed.

The power of forgiveness

When I think of forgiveness I think of mercy. Mercy is when you can forgive and love someone, even when they have done something wrong or hurtful to you. Being merciful is the opposite of hard-heartedness. Forgiveness is a tough one for many of us. We may hold hurts and anger against those who have wronged us in the past.

Remember that our heart hardens when we stay angry and refuse to forgive someone who has hurt us. That hardness of heart can last a lifetime, to our own detriment, and it keeps us bound to the offender, since unless we forgive, we do not forget. The power of forgiveness, on the other hand, can free us from our own self-created bonds with those we believe have hurt or insulted us.

One way to teach forgiveness is to share stories about forgiveness. My children always loved it when I would tell them a story, and I tried to find stories that they could learn from and that illustrated a particular virtue. There are some wonderful stories available, and some sources for these are listed in chapter 8. Here is a story I wrote to illustrate the quality of forgiveness.

Josh and Tony

Josh was eight years old. He was not very big, and Tony, a neighbor boy who was big and tall, thought it was funny to tease Josh just because he was small. Josh did not think it was so funny, and he often ran away from Tony when he saw him coming.

One day Josh was walking home from school, and Tony threw a rock at him. On this day, Josh could not run fast enough, and the rock hit him hard in the back of the head. It knocked him over and made him unconscious.

Josh's mother heard the neighborhood children yelling out in the street, and she looked out the window and saw him lying on the street bleeding. She ran to pick him up and immediately took him to the hospital.

Josh woke up. His head was hurting so badly! Tears ran down his cheeks as the doctor gave him a shot and made five stitches to sew up the wound from the rock. The doctor was very nice, but it still hurt. Josh did not like being at the hospital.

When it was all over and Josh and his mother got home, Josh was very angry with Tony. He had already decided he was never going to forgive Tony, even if Tony said he was sorry.

The doctor was a very nice lady

The next day, Tony and his mother came over. Tony's mom made him apologize to Josh. Josh did not think that Tony really meant it. He nodded at Tony, but he would not look at him and did not say one word to him.

After Tony and his mom left, Josh's mom asked him to sit down and talk with her. Josh was still mad and did not want to talk, but she insisted.

She told Josh that it was very important to forgive, even the people who hurt you! Tony did something stupid, but he did not really want to hurt Josh. She explained that when we do not forgive, we hold on to the thing that happened and it stays with us. If we can forgive, we can forget, and it is over.

She also told Josh about the words that Saint Paul taught us: "As you sow, so shall ye reap." That means that if we say and do negative things, these same things will come back to us at some time in the future. Then we learn what it feels like to be treated that way. It also means that if we are loving and kind, this will also return. Others will at some time be loving and kind to us. Our souls learn this way.

She told him that many times when someone acts unkindly, it is because they are upset about their own lives. Tony was probably feeling bad about himself, and to make himself feel better he did something unkind to Josh.

Josh could understand that. But he was still a little confused. Why did he have to forgive? Why would his mother want him to forgive the kid who had made him hurt so badly?

His mother told him again that when we do not forgive, we continue to hurt inside. We are tied to the person who hurt us.

He said, "But Mom, what Tony did was wrong!"

Josh was confused because he thought that to forgive someone meant that somehow, what they did was all right. And he knew that Tony throwing that rock was not right.

His mother smiled at him and told him that forgiving does not mean we accept that what the person did was right. It was still wrong. To forgive means to realize that the person who hurt us made a mistake.

We all make mistakes sometimes. It does not mean we are bad, just that for one reason or another, we made a mistake. We want to be forgiven when we make mistakes, so we also need to forgive.

Learning to let go of hurts allows them to heal. It is a little like your finger when you get a splinter. It heals only when you get the splinter out of your finger.

Josh's mother reminded him of the line in the Lord's Prayer, "Forgive us our debts as we forgive our debtors." This means that as much as we forgive those who owe us or have hurt us, we will be forgiven for our mistakes. Some people want to seek revenge and get back at the person who hurt them, but that is not God's way.

Josh eating his snack

Josh ate his snack and thought about it. Finally, he got it! Some time in some place, Tony will learn his lesson. But that was not Josh's business. That was Tony's business with his parents and with God. All Josh has to do was to forgive and go on with his own life.

This wasn't easy, but Josh made up his mind that it was better to forgive, and so he did.

Next day, when Josh saw Tony at school, he smiled at him. Tony seemed surprised, but he smiled back. They did not become friends, but Tony never teased him again or threw another rock.

Josh learned that what his mother had said was right—Tony had not really meant to hurt him. And because he had been able to forgive, Josh was free to go on with his life.

6

The Child's Own
Approach to Spirit

Activities and Lessons for Ages 3 to 6

The role of education is to interest the child in an external activity to which he will give all his potential.

—Maria Montessori

Maria Montessori wrote in *The Child in the Church:*

> The child must be permitted to penetrate into his supernatural life with his own peculiar manner. Even in the presence of God the child must remain a child.... Respect for the child's nature, which God Himself demands of us, compels us to search most carefully for those conditions in which children can abandon themselves most easily to God.... The child will reveal to us, in certain moments, how he makes his own approach to God.[1]

How does the child approach God and the inner life of the spirit? What are the conditions under which he best connects with his inner life? Do we actually "teach" spirituality, or do we rather join with the child in a spiritual encounter as we look and listen together?

Sofia Cavalletti explains that there is a strong mystical union between the child and God or spirit that is not entirely dependent on human experience. The encounter brings deep joy. She wrote: "In helping the child's religious [spiritual] life, far from imposing something that is foreign to him, we are responding to the child's silent request: 'Help me to come closer to God by myself.'"[2] Nurturing his connection with spirit is yet another way of bestowing dignity on the child and deepening her joy. After a session of prayer with her young friends, a little girl named Stefania told Cavalletti that "My body is happy!"

As we prepare to share with our children our values and spiritual beliefs, we are faced with some decisions. What are the most essential truths of our beliefs? What do we want to present to our children? How can we present them in age-appropriate ways that honor the child's inherent spiritual nature?

Cavalletti gives us some interesting advice that helps answer these questions. She said, "Give the best to the smallest." She also wrote: "The younger the child the more capable he is of receiving great things and the child is satisfied only with the great and essential things."[3] The most pure, essential teaching of our faith is what we must be prepared to give to our children from the earliest years.

What are the cornerstones of our own beliefs? What is worthy of the profound and pure nature of your little child? It must be the deepest truths clothed in the simplest words and actions. If we cannot define our beliefs in this way, perhaps we ourselves have not gone deep enough. Cavalletti noted that if we do not go deep enough and essential enough, we run the risk of confusing our children.

Help me to learn about God all by myself

The motto of the young child is "Help me to do it myself!" We have all seen a young child struggling to carry a heavy jug of water or a big bag of apples. When we try to help he cries out, "Mine!" It is not what is in the jug or the bag, it is the self-mastery that he is claiming and trying to protect.

If we draw a parallel to the child's spiritual life, his motto in this realm would be, as Cavalletti said, "Help me to come closer to God by myself." Children have their own way of doing this. They can have the experience of a very pure and transcendent level of communion with God when they have a relationship with their inner life. On more than one occasion, children have told me that they have seen Mother Mary or an angel, and I do not doubt that this is true.

For children, spiritual experience goes far beyond mere words or any teaching about the world of spirit. Berryman says they have a personal knowledge of God that is "undifferentiated and mostly nonverbal."[4]

Mystics throughout history have sought to obtain direct experience of the spirit and have struggled to put their experiences into words. Children are similar in their own way. If we want to develop our own inner experience and nurture the spiritual experiences of our children, our job is not so much to talk *about* God but to initiate experiences *with* God. Perhaps we go to a house of worship, enter into meditation or watch a sunset to find the peace and solace of heightened inner experience. If this isn't already a shared experience, be sure to take your child along next time.

What kinds of other activities, lessons and materials will draw your child into deep internal experiences? Before you read on and find some practical suggestions, you might want to ponder these next two questions. As you observe your child in different environments and in different activities, what kinds of experiences seem to bring her calmness and joy? What experiences seem to draw her closer to the spirit?

With young children we cannot simply ask them about their inner life. They cannot tell us about something for which they have no words or concepts. We cannot directly see our children's inner life and its growth in the same way we can see a new tooth or an inch of growth. We have to closely observe and infer what makes our children happy and under what conditions we see a glimmer of the inner light shining through.

Up to this point in the book, I have discussed many general concepts and principles about spirituality that you can apply in your daily life with your child. These principles help to create an environment that will nurture her inherent spiritual nature. In this chapter I will provide some specific examples of lessons and activities you can use to open up the pathways for the unfolding of your child's inner life.

All of the activities in this chapter are designed to provide your child with direct experiences with her inner life. Most of the activities also have a physical component, since children need to be active in order to learn and assimilate. These materials are not simply a way to help the teacher teach better—they are carefully designed to help the child enter into the inner life of the spirit.

Both Cavalletti and Montessori were scientists and scholars. They believed in observing children to determine their spontaneous response to stimuli and in using these discoveries as a basis for education. Accordingly, it is the children themselves, from many nations, who have chosen the lessons I include in this book. It is through observation of children that we have learned that this time alone with the inner life is a basic need of their beings.

Feeling at home in the universe

Spiritually, psychologically, mentally and emotionally, the essence of spirituality is a need to feel connected to something greater than we are. The work of Maria Montessori and Sofia Cavalletti showed that the need for protection and security is one of the sensitive periods of the early years. We are a living part of the universe and our love and the vision of connectedness we offer can help our children feel integrated in the larger whole.

You can make a lesson suitable for either a young child or an older elementary child based on this idea of connection with the universe using a series of pictures depicting successive levels of integration. A great source for all of the images is the Internet. Just collect the pictures, scale them to the size you want and print them in color. You can mount them on cardstock or laminate them for longer use.

Begin with pictures of your child and your family. Here is how it could work, with suggestions of pictures you can use:

- Your child: picture of him or her
- Your child is part of your family: picture of your family
- Your immediate family is part of an extended family, including aunts, uncles, grandparents and cousins on both sides of your family: picture of the extended family
- Your extended family is part of the community in which you live: picture of your town
- Your community is part of your state: map or satellite picture of your state
- Your state is part of your country: map of your nation
- Your country is part of a continent: map of your continent

- Your continent is part of a hemisphere: picture of half of the globe
- Your hemisphere is part of the world: picture of the earth
- The world is part of the solar system: picture of the sun and planets
- Our solar system is part of the Milky Way galaxy: picture of a galaxy
- Our galaxy is part of the universe: picture of deep space showing many galaxies
- Our universe is God's creation: picture of the sun or whatever image could represent this for you

I have done this lesson with children as young as five and as old as young adults in two different ways:

As you describe each relationship in the lesson, have the child lay the pictures out in linear fashion. If you leave the pictures on a nice tray on a work shelf or bookcase, he may wish to repeat the lesson by himself many times over.

The second way is a little more complex. It starts with a small circular picture of the child and the family to place in the center and successively larger circular pictures for each expanded level. As you speak about each level, lift the pictures to insert the next one underneath. At the end of the lesson, you will see concentric circles representing ever-larger circles of awareness.

Children love to go out and watch the stars at night. They are quite capable of imagining their part in something infinitely larger than they are. Your child's connection to spirit will take a leap from himself in his house to the entire creation and back again with this lesson.

My quiet space

Early childhood is a stage when a child can have his first personal space dedicated to quiet reflection and meditation. This special place can become a refuge, a place to go for prayer, quiet meditations and talks with God, and an anchor point for the child's spiritual life. It can be quite simple. The important thing is that this is the child's space, and he should take an active role with you in setting it up and choosing the items to place there.

Some prefer to call this space an altar. I love to consider the meaning of the word *altar* and its similarity to the word *alter*, which means "to change." An altar, then, is a place of alteration, or change—a place where we are changed by our contact with spirit.

Start with a small table or even a box at a convenient height for the child. Have a small chair or a cushion the child can sit on in front of it. The little shelf or table should be located in a place where the child can go when he or she wishes and where he can be relatively undisturbed during his quiet times. It can also be used as a place where you sit together and talk about your beliefs.

You might have a selection of colored cloths for the child to choose from to cover the table. Place on the table a special picture of your highest representation of the creator, a child's Bible or some objects you consider sacred.

You might include special objects from nature such as a flower or shell that the child especially likes. This is a working space that can change as your child desires to place new objects on it that mean something to him.

Part of the process of nurturing your child's inner life is to

respect its internal cycles and observe how it operates. You are
helping your child create a time and space for the inner life, not
requiring that inner life to operate on a specific schedule. The
times your child spends in this space may be exceedingly brief
or more extended as she discovers the richness of silence.

On the next page, we see two examples of children's quiet
spaces. In the first picture, a child picked some roses and
wanted to give one to each of the children in her classroom. The
space reflects the joy and generosity of her heart. In the second
picture, we see an altar in a more traditional religious style.

Prayer

Our job is to provide children with experiences and materials that will lead them to enter into communion with their
own inner teacher, the voice of conscience, and with God.
Prayer is one vital means of communion.

Think about prayer as a cycle. You may pray as an expression of love and gratitude to the source of life. You may pray
for guidance or healing for yourself or a loved one. Whatever
your reasons may be, you are sending your energy to God by
directing your prayer "upwards." That is the first half of the
cycle.

In the second half of the cycle, you receive the blessing
of God's energy coming back to you. It is the return current
of God's love to your heart that completes the cycle. Prayer
can become a habit, a powerful tool you can model and teach
your child. Developing a ritual of daily prayer can provide a
comforting and sustaining rhythm of going to the divine source
each and every day.

Cavalletti noted that when praying spontaneously, children

Two examples of children's quiet spaces

A small table with a tablecloth, a pitcher filled with flowers and a basket of smaller glass vases. On the right is a tray with utensils for trimming the stems of the flowers and pouring water into the individual vases. This space shows an activity for a child who feels the joy of beautiful flowers and would like to share one with each family member or classmate.

An altar in a more traditional style, with a candle, a Bible, a small card with a quote to meditate on and a small statue of Jesus. Notice the baskets below and to the side of the table containing other possible altar items. The child chose the items she wanted to set up for that particular day for her quiet, meditative time.

in the early years of life always pray as praise. They don't ask for things when they pray, they simply thank God. They will tell God that they love their parents. They will thank God for the beautiful day, for the lovely meal that Mommy cooked, and on and on.

Children do not begin to ask God for anything until they reach the reasoning mind and the new stage of moral questioning that begins at the same time. Ask a four- or five-year-old what he wants to pray about and he will very likely tell you he wants to thank God for his family, his pet, his bicycle. This is normal and to be encouraged. Allow your child to evolve through his own cycle of prayer on his own inner timeline, and avoid prematurely teaching your child to ask for things in his prayers.

I used to ask the children in my preschool class what they were grateful for each Thanksgiving. I would write the word *Thanksgiving* on a big piece of paper, cut it in half and reverse the order of the two halves, so that the children could see more clearly that it means *giving thanks*. I remember one little four-year-old who answered that she was most thankful for her mommy and daddy and her new bicycle. Children are grateful for what is right in front of them and for those who love them. Perhaps this is a clue as to how they see God—as Elisabeth Caspari liked to see him—as "God with two feet."

Affirmations

Many religious traditions include verbal prayers and recitations, and they invoke a devotional aspect all their own. You and your child might wish to learn some formal prayers, such as "The Lord's Prayer," the "Hail Mary" or a Buddhist chant.

Positive affirmations are an engaging and popular way to affirm the basic goodness of your child and help him see himself in a more positive light and to improve his state of mind. You can teach your child to say, "I am joy!" or "I am love," "God loves me!" or whatever you feel is appropriate. We so often affirm the negatives in our lives: "I'm so tired," or "I'm so poor," while it is so easy to learn to affirm the positive instead.

These positive affirmations plant seeds in the mind of a positive outlook on life. We all know that some see the glass half-full while others see it half-empty. With the use of our positive words and the power of the subconscious, we can help our children affirm and see in their mind's eye the glass as at least half-full!

Meditation

There are many other ways you can promote your child's communion with God. Meditation is an important one. Become an observer of your child. When you see your child at peace and quiet, do not interrupt. Let his concentration, which is a form of meditation, become a habit.

Sometimes we see the child relax into a meditative state during or after playing some simple game, being by herself in her crib or in her play yard or on the living room couch. Concentration is an important quality of life, and children learn it best when they can have uninterrupted work and play times in quiet, peaceful environments. All children need periods of active physical play alternating with quiet play.

You can teach simple meditation by playing a piece of soothing music (the largo or very slow movement of classical pieces is especially effective), doing some rhythmic breathing and just sitting in stillness for a few minutes. Many children love to do this.

Montessori developed a game called the Silence Game as she learned that children enjoy silence. To play the Silence Game, pick a time when you think the children might succeed in sitting in silence, and ask them to sit quietly with you. Begin to call their attention to their feet by asking if they can keep their feet very still, then their hands, and finally if they can keep their breathing quiet. Very quietly invite them to listen to the sounds in the environment that they may not have noticed.

Maintain the stillness only as long as the children are inclined. Then quietly ask your child or children, one at a time, to come sit by you when you whisper their names. It is a lovely experience that can last two or three minutes, and sometimes substantially longer.

Quiet time is important for the soul. It is important for us as adults and for our children. It is easy to drown out the still, small voice within when we are always busy, always doing and going, or the radio or television is playing. In addition to planned quiet times, provide time for walks and outside time in all seasons, both during the day and at night.

Yoga for children

A very fun and relaxing activity with children is yoga. Many schools have adopted yoga as part of physical education programs, as it helps children to relax and get centered as well as develop strength and flexibility. Some families like to practice yoga together.

Many of the postures are simple, while others are more challenging. You will very likely find that your child can do those challenging ones more easily than you can!

Children practicing yoga

Yoga cards with pictures of simple positions children can imitate are available for purchase. You can put these in a basket near the child's altar or work space for her to use whenever she may wish.

Learning to observe

I have often played a game with children where I ask one child to come stand in front of the class for a minute or two, not telling the class why. Then I ask him to go into another room, and I begin asking the rest of the class questions about the colors of his clothing, what kind of shoes he wore, and so forth.

The first time we tried this, I was a little amazed at how few of the children noticed the details of how their friend was dressed. So over the weeks we would practice now and then, with children getting sharper and noticing more each time.

I extended the game into a new activity by bringing a basket of objects covered with a scarf. I would lay them out, name them and then quickly cover them with the scarf and ask the children to take turns naming the items in order. This is a skill that children can get very good at.

Another variation of this activity is to collect a pile of picture cards. As you lay out each card make up a story that connects the pictures. Many children can remember four or five, some seven or eight. One little boy named Chester could recall up to fifty pictures, all in the right order.

Nicholas Roerich, prolific artist, anthropologist and author, wrote about the need for children to learn to observe to help in opening their spirits:

> Begin the refinement of observation upon everyday objects. It would be a mistake to direct the pupils too rapidly to higher concepts.... We can propose that the pupil pass through an unfamiliar room at a run and yet with concentrated observation.... Children are very fond of such tasks.... The most ordinary routines can become the gateway to the most complex. Imagine the exultation of a child when he exclaims, "I've seen more!"[5]

Scripture

For many of us, our scriptures represent the Word of God. They are absolutely essential to our idea of spiritual education and the development of our child's inner life. Whatever your spiritual background may be, the sacred scriptures of your faith are a good place to start. We will provide examples primarily from a Christian background in this chapter, since that is what many of the readers of this book are likely to be familiar with.

If you are from a different background or would like to introduce teachings from other spiritual traditions to your child, the
principles used to develop these activities can be readily applied
to the source material from those traditions.*

There are many simple Bible story picture books you can
use to familiarize your child with stories from both the Old and
the New Testaments. Everyone, including children, loves a good
story, and the Bible is a compendium of amazing stories.

The Bible Story, by Arthur S. Maxwell, a ten-volume set of
stories of the Bible for children, is an excellent choice as your
child gets a little older. It tells the basic stories in a way that
is suitable for any denomination. The lives of Jesus and other
figures in the Old and New Testaments provide a rich resource
for teaching spiritual principles.

Here is an example of how you can create materials to
illustrate stories from the Bible and make them come alive for
your child. This series is based on the narratives of the birth of
Christ found in the books of Luke and Matthew. The sequence
can be used in the weeks leading up to and following Christmas.

You will need some basic Nativity scene pieces and something to use as a backdrop, which can be as simple as a colored
shoe box, to represent the setting for each scene in the sequence.
At Christmas time I shopped around for inexpensive plastic or
ceramic figurines that I could use. It is possible to buy complete
readymade sets of these materials from a number of groups
associated with the Catechesis of the Good Shepherd, the
organization founded in America by Sofia Cavalletti. (Search

* For children's stories from the life of Gautama Buddha, one good source is *Prince
Siddhartha: The Story of Buddha*, by Jonathan Landaw and Janet Brooke. There are
also illustrated children's books based on the Jataka tales, which teach children simple
moral lessons. The two-volume set *The Story of Sri Krishna for Children*, by Swami
Raghaveshananda, is a good resource for stories from the Hindu tradition.

the Internet for "Catechesis of the Good Shepherd.")

Another way to work with the stories is with simple dress-up props. Children are able to create elaborate stories in their play with their dolls or action figures and whatever materials may be at hand. If you can enter in to the sense of imagination with the child, the story can be very engaging without the need for elaborate props.

If your child is an independent reader, you may wish to make a little booklet of the scripture to go with each lesson. The booklet can be as simple or sophisticated as you wish. You can write the text and do a drawing for each page. You can input the text and print it out with or without illustrations. Then staple the pages together. When I was making a lot of books for my classroom, I got complimentary wallpaper sample books from local stores that I could use for sturdy covers.

The chart on the following pages shows the six episodes in the Infancy Narrative Cycle with corresponding Bible verses and material used to illustrate the stories. The photographs show materials from several different sources. Some figures are store-bought; others were molded by hand in clay or rendered in wood. The backgrounds are simple boxes or scenes hand-painted on wood.

Steps in presenting each episode

The sequence of steps to present each story was carefully developed over many years based on the responses of hundreds of children. It is designed to first introduce the basic story and initiate some discussion about the major theme. Then, when you read the scripture, the child is ready to listen with a sense of interest and relevance to his own life. Following the reading

The Infancy Narrative Cycle

1.
The Annunciation
Luke 1:26–38

Mary's house

Materials:
Mary, Archangel
Gabriel

2.
The Visitation
Luke 1:39–56

Elisabeth's house

Materials:
Mary, Elisabeth

3.
**The Birth of
Jesus and the
Adoration of
the Shepherds**
Luke 2:1–20

The stable

Materials:
manger,
Holy Family,
shepherds and
sheep, other
animals

The Infancy Narrative Cycle

4.
**The Adoration
of the Magi**
Matthew 2:1–12

The stable

Materials:
manger,
Holy Family,
angel,
three wise men
(with camels if
desired)

5.
**The Presentation
in the Temple**
Luke 2:21–33,
   36–39

The Temple

Materials:
Holy Family,
basket with
doves, Simeon,
Anna

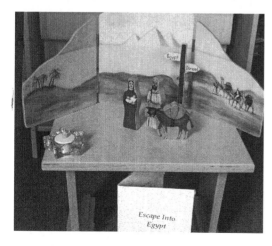

6.
**The Escape
into Egypt**
Matthew 2:13–23

Mary and
Joseph's house

Materials:
angel, Holy
Family, donkey

we provide concrete materials that allow the child opportunity to meditate with the content of the scripture and process it in his or her own way.

1. Narrate the story briefly in your own words, following the Bible account and without embellishing. Invite your child to think about what this event might mean to him and to the world. The material is not present for this initial telling of the story.

2. Light a candle to honor the sacredness of scripture.

3. Read the Bible passage. If the child is not familiar with some of the words in the story, explain them as you read.

4. Show the materials you have made that will help the child understand the story and allow her to think about its meaning. Tell the story again in your own words, but as closely to the actual words of the passage as you can recall, this time setting up and moving the materials as the story unfolds. The child may want to repeat the lesson at this time.

5. Permit time for spontaneous prayer, offering a line or two from the narrative that may be conducive for use in a prayer.

6. Show the little booklet of scripture, if you have one and if your child can read. Invite your child to use the material with the booklet, if desired.

7. Place the lesson on a shelf and allow your child to return to it as often as he desires.

8. After a period of work, which may occur over a few hours or a few days, invite your child to draw a picture of the story.

9. Periodically, over the weeks and months of your child's work with the material, invite her to draw more pictures

of the story. You may see interesting features appear in the art that reflect her growing understanding.

These same steps can be used to illustrate any episode in the life of Jesus. For example, the events of Easter week, beginning with Palm Sunday and ending with the resurrection on Easter Sunday, can be presented in that season. The miracles of Jesus and many of the parables also make wonderful stories for children (more on parables in chapter 7).

This same set of steps could be used to illustrate episodes from the lives of other figures from the Bible, of Buddha or of any of the saints of East or West. Take the principles contained in these activities and adapt them to your own spiritual path. As you make the stories real for your child at this age, you provide a foundation for the deeper teachings of your faith that the child will learn in later years.

No matter what your spiritual beliefs, share them with your children. You can draw on any faith-based experience or any form of spirituality. One reason your children came to you was for the truth and wisdom you can pass on to them. Share your heart with them! They will always remember.

The following pages in this chapter cover some additional ideas for presenting spiritual principles in ways that are meaningful and engaging for a preschool child.

A special prayer

Help your child find her own special prayer or song to feel close to her inner life and the love in her heart. It might be an existing prayer such as "The Lord's Prayer" or something as simple as "O God, you are so magnificent" or "God is love and I am love."

Songs

Music is a joyful way to celebrate your spirituality and the traditions of your family heritage. Sing to your child and sing with your child. For my children it was the song, "You Are My Sunshine." I changed it a little to be "You are my sweetie, my special sweetie...." This was a sign of my undying love for them and every now and then, in their twenties and thirties they still remember how special it made them feel.

Another song even two- and three-year-olds can sing is "I Am Loving and Kind," which is set to the tune of the refrain from "Home on the Range."

I Am Loving and Kind

First verse (point to your heart)

I am loving and kind
I am loving and kind
I am loving and kind all the time. *(2 times)*

Second verse (gesture toward each child with open palm)

You are loving and kind
You are loving and kind
You are loving and kind all the time. *(2 times)*

Third verse (hold hands)

We are loving and kind
We are loving and kind
We are loving and kind all the time. *(2 times)*

Matching cards and the three-period lesson

Children respond to images. There is a very simple activity you can use with any images in a specific category you wish to introduce to your child. It involves sets of duplicate pictures that the child can match in rows and learn new vocabulary.

However you conceptualize spirituality and the inner life, you can use images that correspond to those ideas. For example, if you wish to teach the fundamentals of Christianity, you could collect pictures of the life of Christ or other episodes from the Bible. If you wish to introduce your child to the religions of the world, you might collect pictures of the world's great spiritual teachers or the symbols of those religions. On the next page is an example of matching cards for symbols of the world's major religions, readily available online.

Print two color copies of each image directly onto card stock or on regular paper which is then mounted on card stock. Standard 3½" x 5" note cards work well and are sturdy enough for repeated use. The cards should all be the same size. You may wish to laminate them for long-term use. Office supply stores often have laminators that you can use at minimal expense.

You can also make matching labels for each symbol if you wish. Affix one label to the bottom of one of the cards in the set. The second label in the set is loose.

Steps in presentation

Choose a place where you and your child can work with the cards undisturbed. A nice, clean area rug is good, since it is easy for your child to pick up and move the cards on the soft surface and he can get comfortable on the floor. An uncluttered

Matching Cards for World Religions

Christianity

Judaism

Islam

Matching Cards for World Religions

Buddhism

Hinduism

Taoism

table space works well too. In the first introductory work, you can just make it a picture matching exercise.

1. Lay one set of cards out in a vertical column to the left of the work area.
2. Lay the second set at random off to the right. Match one pair of pictures and invite your child to match the others.

The three-period lesson

Either before or after the matching work, you can use one set of the pictures and introduce the vocabulary using a simple technique called the three-period lesson. The three-period lesson is a simple way you can teach any kind of vocabulary. The basic steps are:

1. "This is..."
2. "Please show me..." and
3. "What is this?"

Here are the steps in the three-period lesson:

Introduction: Tell your child that you are going to be seeing some pictures that are signs of the world's great religions. "People all over the world believe in God in different ways and these beautiful pictures show us something important to the believers of these religions."

1. **This is:** Place one picture on an uncluttered surface and say the name of the image: "This is the sign for Christianity. Can you say Christianity?" Put out a second picture next to the first. "This is the sign for Judaism. Can you say Judaism?" Put out a third picture. "This is

the sign for Islam. Can you say Islam?" Continue in this manner through the remaining cards. This is the first period, which is simply a naming activity.

2. **Please show me:** For the second period, ask the child: "Can you please show me the sign for Christianity?" Wait for the child to point at the cross. "Can you please show me the sign for Islam?" "Can you please show me the sign for Judaism?" Mix the pictures up and ask a few more times, varying your questions. "Can you please put the sign for Christianity here?" "Can you please put the sign for Judaism here?"

3. **What is this?** The third period is to show a picture and ask, "What is this?"

Using labels

The next step is to work with the loose labels, as shown in the illustration on the next page. The child matches a set of pictures and then finds the appropriate label. It is rather amazing, but even a child who cannot read can match the labels by carefully examining the letters in each word. It is a useful step on the road to learning to read.

A further step in using matching cards is to also use them to teach simple facts about the pictures. This step can be added when the child is familiar with all of the pictures and the names.

You can make sets of matching pictures about almost anything you choose: the stages of the life of Christ, favorite flowers from seed packets, or anything that is beautiful and uplifting for your child. I collect duplicate sets of postcards of monuments, state flowers and beautiful works of art in museums and churches wherever I go. Montessorian Aline Wolf developed an entire art appreciation program for children using

A child working with matching cards. The cards
on the left have labels attached. The ones on the
right have labels separate from the cards.

duplicate sets of art cards. You are building a foundation of images and words for later when children want to know more.

If you analyze the word *imagination*, it comes from the Latin root *imago*, or "image." We are fueling the child's imagination as well as building general knowledge and vocabulary with these cards.

You can also use these same pictures with older children. Once the child is in the stage of the reasoning mind, can read and becomes hungry for facts, type out an explanation or story card for each image. In this new activity, the child lays out the pictures, the loose labels and the story cards. He matches the labels under each picture then reads the story card and places it next to the appropriate image.

Vocabulary for prayer

Familiarize your child with a vocabulary for prayer. Based on your understanding and beliefs, introduce new words that describe your own inner experience and the praise of life.

For example, Isaiah 9:6 contains many names for Christ. Each one of these names may be the impetus to spontaneous prayer in the heart of the child.

> *For unto us a child is born, unto us a son is given,*
> *and the government will be on his shoulders.*
> *And he will be called Wonderful Counselor,*
> *Mighty God, Everlasting Father,*
> *the Prince of Peace.*

After your child learns these words, you can play Handel's Messiah and listen for these same words being sung. Cavalletti had long experience with making sets of cards with one of these phrases on each card. Children loved to carry them around in processions and make their own copies of them.

There are some wonderful children's books on spiritual themes that you can use to introduce new words. I particularly like books on the world religions because I find children love to find out about other children and how they live. One especially good book is *A Faith Like Mine*, by Laura Buller.

Angels

You may also wish to teach your child about angels. Children often have deep spiritual experiences with forces we cannot see. They love to hear the magnificent stories of the intercession of angels in the lives of people, as these stories may well parallel their own inner experiences.

Joan Wester Anderson has written a wonderful series of books of reportedly true stories about angels. Especially good for children are the stories of other children's experiences with angels in *An Angel to Watch Over Me: True Stories of Children's Encounters with Angels.*

After you share such a story, invite your child's comments. If he has something to share with you about his own inner life or his own experiences, this may be the time it will come forth. If this happens it is important to listen with an open heart.

A wonderful follow up to angel stories or any stories at all is to give the child materials for creating and expressing her perceptions through art.

This child is making a jeweled crown as a
meditation on the halo of the saints.

7

Using Parables to Reveal
Spiritual Mysteries

While definitions circumscribe and limit us,
parables open us to the mysteries of spirit.
—Mary Ellen Maunz

As we examine the teachings of Jesus and other great world teachers, we find that it was quite common for them to teach with parables. In Matthew 13, it is recorded that Jesus explained how he used parables very deliberately to reveal spiritual mysteries to those who have ears to hear.

Parables are a uniquely spiritual method of teaching. The parable is an open invitation to meditate upon spiritual concepts. It has the unique capacity of keeping us from going astray. It has, as it were, two rails that keep the mind on track, these rails being the two simultaneous levels in a parable.

Take, for example, the parable of the leaven. The parable is very simple: "The kingdom of heaven is like unto leaven, which a woman took, and hid in three measures of meal."[1] The first rail of the parable gives us a woman in the mundane action of baking bread. But on the second rail there is the possibility to experience the transcendent nature of the kingdom of heaven.

While definitions circumscribe and limit us, parables open us to the mysteries of God. We can go into them just as deeply as we are able. Children understand this method. They go deeper than one might imagine, particularly if they are given the time and the materials to think deeply. I have seen children kneading dough and watching it rise as the activity for this parable. When asked what they are doing, they simply say they are watching the kingdom of heaven grow.

One of the most beautiful lessons Montessori developed is now used all over the world by people with many different beliefs and situations in life, from preschools to hospitals. It is the presentation of the parable of the Good Shepherd. One reason it is so popular is because children of every faith in nearly every nation on earth can relate to it. Let us consider how the Good Shepherd might meet the needs of the souls of so many children.

The Good Shepherd

The parable of the Good Shepherd is found in chapter 10 of the Gospel of John. (Several passages about the wolf and the hireling have been omitted from this version so that it would be suitable for initial work with young children.)

The Good Shepherd

Truly, truly, I say to you, He that enters not by the door into the sheepfold, but climbs in some other way, he is a thief and a robber.

But he that enters in by the door is the shepherd of the sheep. To him will the porter open the gate, and the sheep hear his voice: and he calls his own sheep by name, and leads them out.

And when he takes out his own sheep, he goes before them, and the sheep follow him: for they know his voice. And they will not follow a stranger, but will run away from him: for they do not know the voice of strangers.

Jesus spoke this parable to them: but they did not

understand what he told them.

Then Jesus said to them again, truly, truly, I say to you, I am the open door of the sheep. All that ever came before me are thieves and robbers: but the sheep did not hear them.

I am the open door: if any man enter in by me, he shall be saved, and shall go in and out, and find pasture. I am come that they might have life, and that they might have it more abundantly.

I am the good shepherd: the good shepherd gives his life for the sheep. I am the good shepherd, and I know my sheep, and my sheep know me. As the Father knows me, even so know I the Father: and I lay down my life for the sheep.

And I have other sheep, which are not of this pasture: them also I must bring home, and they shall hear my voice; and there shall be one pasture, and one shepherd.

The theme of the Good Shepherd is also found in the parable of the lost sheep, from Luke, chapter 15, verses 4–7, and these two parables are often taught together.

The Lost Sheep

What man of you, having an hundred sheep, if he lose one of them, does not leave the ninety and nine in the wilderness, and go after that which is lost, until he find it?

And when he has found it, he lays it on his shoulders, rejoicing. And when he comes home, he calls together his friends and neighbors, saying unto them,

Rejoice with me; for I have found my sheep which was lost.

I say unto you, that likewise joy shall be in heaven over one sinner that repents, more than over ninety and nine just persons, which need no repentance.

There are many representations of Christ in the Bible: the infant messiah, the young boy of twelve speaking before the doctors, the teacher of the multitudes, the one executing judgment. Which one is best for the child to relate to?

The baby is not a figure of authority to a child. The boy of twelve may well be used as a role model for a pre-teen preparing for confirmation, but it is not necessarily appropriate for children in general. Judgment is a sophisticated concept for a young child, and does not offer the security of a guiding figure. Some children may have had negative associations with teachers, so this may not always be best.

For most children, the idea of a shepherd is a neutral image. And because the concept of a figure to lead us safely is not unique to Christianity, this parable is acceptable to people of many religions. The Good Shepherd, as this image is depicted in John's Gospel, is well suited to the spiritual and psychological needs of children of many ages.

To present the parable with maximum effect for the child, it is useful to buy or make a set of the figures to depict the story visually. In addition to a figure to represent the Good Shepherd, you will need a sheepfold and a set of a dozen or so sheep, as shown in photograph on the next page.

Cavalletti recommends that these figures be made out of wood as two-dimensional figures that can stand on a small base. Her concept is that three-dimensional figures should

Materials for presenting the parable of the Good Shepherd

be used for historical personages and two-dimensional figures for parables. In this way the child sees a concrete difference between the characters in the parables and the historical figures such as we saw in the Infancy Narratives.

How to present the parables for children 2½ to 6

The presentation for any parable follows the same general format as was outlined in chapter 6, allowing you to tell the story three times during the initial presentation. This allows the essentials of the story to sink in. These are the steps for presenting this parable:

- Begin by calling the child's attention to the fact that you have a story to tell. For example, in the parable of the Good Shepherd, Jesus' followers asked him who he really was. He explained with this story.

- Tell the story in your own words. You can abbreviate the parable somewhat as long as you include the key features. For young children, we leave out the character of the wolf and the hireling, as was done in the version above.
  - You may wish to add the story of the Lost Sheep as part of the parable of the Good Shepherd.
- Discuss the story with your child, emphasizing that there is a mystery for us to understand. Here is the most important point of all: **Do *not* try to explain the meaning,** but rather allow your child to meditate and consider what it means. This process of understanding the mystery may unfold over time and may even last for years.
  - Light a candle and read the original text of the parable from the Bible.
  - Introduce the figures and other material illustrating the story, and tell the story again in your own words, moving the figurines to act it out.
  - If you have one available, offer the child a little booklet with the words of the parable.
  - Allow your child to play with the figures, acting out the story herself.
  - After your child has worked with the figures, invite her to do a drawing of the parable. This is an important step in this process. Cavalletti called these "theological drawings." Many times you will see that the child's understanding will take a leap as she is expressing herself through drawing.

Here is the story as I might tell it, integrating the parable of the lost sheep with the Good Shepherd right from the beginning.

I have a story to tell you—are you ready to listen?
A long time ago people wanted to know who Jesus really was. He spoke such beautiful teachings and he was so kind to all of the people and he could heal. Many of us still ask in our prayers for Jesus to show us in our heart all that he is.

One day, while Jesus was still walking among them, the people asked him who he was. He gave them a mysterious answer.

"I am the Good Shepherd"—not just any shepherd, but the "Good" shepherd.

The Good Shepherd knows each and every sheep by name. I wonder how many sheep he had in his flock. So many names he must know! What can it mean?

The sheep listen for him and always know his voice. They come when he calls, and if another voice tries to call them away, they will not go, because they love the Good Shepherd and will follow him.

The shepherd knows all their needs: he leads them out each morning to the lovely meadows where there are green grasses to eat and still blue waters to drink. He speaks to each of them, lovingly calling them by name.

When it is time to return, the Good Shepherd leads them safely back to the sheepfold for their rest. He checks that each one is there, because he knows each one by name.

One evening he noticed that one of his sheep was missing. Oh no! What do you think he did? Did he have so many sheep that he did not need an extra one?

Oh no! He knew exactly which one was missing. After he

made sure all the others were safe in the sheepfold, he went looking. He walked back calling the little lamb's name over and over. He walked miles back to where the sheep had fallen into a bush and was stuck. As soon as the sheep heard his shepherd's voice, he bleated and the shepherd found him.

The shepherd was so joyful to find the lost sheep. He hugged him to his heart and carried him home because the little sheep was cold and tired and afraid.

When they returned to the sheepfold, the shepherd once again counted all his sheep until he was sure they were all there. Then, he was so full of joy that he had found his lost sheep he gathered all his friends and celebrated with a little party!

How much the shepherd loves his sheep!

When it is time to sleep, he lays his body in front of the gate to sleep (with one eye open!) so they will be safe during the night.

I wonder how many sheep the Good Shepherd has in his pasture? Are they all in just one pasture and one flock? How far does the voice of the Good Shepherd reach?

Jesus told us the answer. He said he has many sheep in many flocks! He knows their names also and they, too, listen to his voice. And one day, there will be one shepherd and one flock.

He also told us that just as much as his father, God, loves him, that is how much he loves his sheep.

What can he mean with such beautiful words?

When the story has been told, I take a few moments and gently ask the children about the story and permit them to share their first responses and their questions. I might go back to key points and ask what they think it might mean. This may last just a few minutes or longer, depending on the children's interest in talking about it.

Now it is time for reading the original source material. To give a special emphasis to the holiness of scripture, I like to light a candle on the small table where I am seated when I tell the story. I read John 10:2–7, 9, 10–11 (starting with "I am come") and 14–17, and Luke 15:4–7.

Next it is time to show the materials. I let the children know that I have something very special for them to help them think about the story. First I bring the sheepfold and place it on the table. Then I slowly and deliberately take the shepherd and each one of the sheep out of the attractive box or basket where they are stored and place them inside the sheepfold.

Once all the figures are on the table, I retell the story. This time I move the figures slowly as I tell the story. It is utterly amazing how these actions will rivet the attention of children—and adults! When I get to the part where I am moving all the

Demonstrating the presentation in 1992 for a large group of adults

sheep out to their pasture, as unobtrusively as I can, I put one of the sheep in my lap. After all the other sheep are back in the sheepfold, the Good Shepherd goes back to find that one lost sheep.

After the story is complete I carefully put the figures back in their basket or box. I show the children where the figures will live on our work shelf and invite the children to select the Good Shepherd whenever they wish to work with it.

This is usually enough for the purposes of the lesson. I may bring it out another day and show the booklet that contains the words of the parable. Children who can read may read it and then move the figures. Some children like to make their own booklets and decorate them with their special drawings. Your child may wish to dramatize the story in a play with costumes. All of these activities help children to assimilate and internalize the presence of the Good Shepherd in their lives.

This story has a deep resonance for many children. A mother sent my colleague and me a letter after the presentation of the Good Shepherd that we had given to her five-year-old adopted daughter. Just the night before, she had confronted a painful question as to why her birth mother had left her, and her mother and father had spent the evening telling the story and reassuring her of her place in their family. Here is an excerpt from that letter.

She had the first lessons on the Good Shepherd on Thursday. She went home that night and played with her little lamby, who kept getting lost and then found by her....

Most miraculous, she started a ritual with the Good Shepherd story. Last evening as we were getting ready for bed, I peeked in her room and she had set up a little fenced area, two areas of green felt (outside the fence the green felt had a strip of blue going through it), a group of sheep (from two nativity sets and Playmobil toys) and the good shepherd statue we have.

I sat down quietly next to her and she told the Good Shepherd story almost *word for word* with the slow, gentle tone of voice and movements that were demonstrated in the lesson. It was miraculous. She told the story with all the movements twice.

She woke up this morning and wanted to have all the material on her bed. I found a large piece of poster board and put it on her bed, and she set it up all again and re-enacted the story. She added a "wolf" this morning (who was another stuffed lamb).

Then she said, "I want to do the Good Shepherd story every day, Mom."

I cannot thank you enough for making the beautiful materials and presenting the lesson in such a dramatic, yet peaceful way.

Your child may also be interested in other activities having to do with this parable. The Twenty-Third Psalm is also frequently used with the parable. It speaks of the shepherd and explains the roles of the Good Shepherd in our lives. This psalm can be used as a passage that the children memorize and recite. It can also be used as a starting point for art work to illustrate the role of the Good Shepherd.

The Twenty-Third Psalm

The Lord is my shepherd; I shall not want.

He causes me to lie down in green pastures; he leads me beside still waters.

He restores my soul; he leads me in paths of righteousness for his name's sake.

Even when I walk in the valley of darkness, I will fear no evil: for you are with me, your rod and your staff, they comfort me.

You set a table before me in the presence of my enemies: you anoint my head with oil; my cup overflows.

May only goodness and kindness pursue me all the days of my life, and I will dwell in the house of the Lord forever.

The material for the parable of the Good Shepherd is something that can remain in your home or classroom for years. Children will go to it again and again as they get older, finding deeper layers of meaning. For example, one fine day you may see the children spontaneously begin to draw children in the place of sheep. They come to their own inner realization that the sheep represent the souls of men. How much better it is for children's inner growth when they arrive at this insight rather than if we tell them and deprive them of the mysterious unfolding of understanding.

You can develop many more activities for your child focusing on the Good Shepherd, such as the craft project shown below. On the upper right of the table you can see small baskets containing pre-cut paper sheep and sections of fence with a glue stick. There are also sheets of green paper in the larger basket

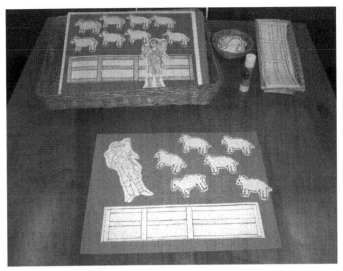

A craft project for the parable of the Good Shepherd

for the child to choose as his background. The child can color the pieces, glue them onto the paper and perhaps glue on cotton balls to make the sheep fluffy.

How the Good Shepherd meets the needs of children from 2½ to 6

For children from the ages of 2½ to 6, the parable of the Good Shepherd provides a profound sense of peace and safety. It answers the spiritual and psychological need for security and protection that Maria Montessori identified as a sensitive period in the young child's development. As children work with the materials, they spontaneously associate the figure of the Good Shepherd with light and love. The theological drawings of children that show the Good Shepherd with a flame or hearts on his breast reveal this connection.

The concept that the Good Shepherd speaks and the sheep

listen and recognize his voice is very important to the child. The Good Shepherd knows each sheep by name, giving the child the sense that the love of God is extremely personal.

Jerome Berryman has used the parable with terminally ill children, bringing felt figures with Velcro on a green felt background so that even a child in bed can hear the message and work with the figures. Peace and security is especially important for these children who are coping with their imminent death. They respond deeply to the love the Good Shepherd has for his sheep.

Once this initial stage of the work has been completed, the theological drawings begin to reveal deeper levels of understanding. The children will spontaneously begin to draw children's faces on the lambs. They may suddenly understand that the Shepherd is Jesus. If you are Christian and wish to pursue this line of understanding, another sequence of lessons can transition to the sheep being replaced by figurines of people and the Good Shepherd being replaced by a figure of Jesus and eventually by the elements of bread and wine on a Communion table.

How the Good Shepherd meets the needs of children from 6 to 10

Children from 6 to 10, who are entering a stage of moral development, are reassured to hear of the lost sheep and to know that God loves us whether we are naughty or good. Even if we stray for a time, the Good Shepherd will come to look for us and bring us home, not for punishment but for celebration.

The association with light and love deepens as children begin to understand that there is a gift that the Good Shepherd gives to them personally—a private relationship that they can develop with him.

How the Good Shepherd meets the needs of children from 10 and up

Children aged 10 to 12 years and even older focus on the element of the story where the Good Shepherd leads the sheep toward green grass and crystal water. Their need is for the sense of inner guidance in exploring the wider world, and they see that the Good Shepherd leads them forward to what is good for them. When they are guided by the shepherd, they are safe and their needs are met.

As adults many of us still love to read the parable and meditate on its meaning in our own lives.

Deepening your child's spiritual experience

Cavalletti's work with children from three to twelve has revealed four major features of the child's spiritual experience with the parables:

1. The child's experience of joy and understanding is spontaneous rather than in response to an adult's prompting.
2. The experience is complex—involving feeling, thinking and moral consciousness.
3. The experience is not limited to cultural conditioning.
4. The experience is deep.

The child's spiritual and religious life is a reality. We can learn to help our children more effectively as we understand more about how they learn and what resonates with them.

Other parables

While the parable of the Good Shepherd can be central to a program of spiritual growth for a child, other parables, such as those found in Matthew 13, may also be taught with this method.

- The Kingdom of Heaven and the Grain. *v. 13:24–30*
- The Mustard Seed. *v. 13:31–32*
- The Leaven. *v. 13:33*
- The Sower. *v. 13:38*
- The Tares and the Wheat. *v. 13:37–43*
- The Pearl of Great Price. *v. 13:45–46*
- The Net. *v. 13:47–50*

Materials used for presenting the parables of The Pearl of Great Price (above) and The Grain (below)

How do you know if these spiritual lessons and experiences are deepening your child's spirituality? Cavalletti says we can expect to see measurable growth in four ways:

1. Your child will express a deep, abiding joy.
2. A mysterious knowledge will arise in your child, going beyond what you have taught.
3. Your child will be in awe of the invisible or nonmaterial meanings of existence.
4. Your child will develop a capacity for deep, personal prayer that expresses itself in praise.

This program is described more fully in *The Child in the Church*, by Maria Montessori, and in the books of Sofia Cavalletti. *The Religious Potential of the Child*, by Cavalletti, is especially rich. By searching the words "Catechesis of the Good Shepherd" online you can find many national organizations that use this system of teaching and offer additional information, resources and training. Although originally developed for Catholic children, the principles that underlie the system can be adapted to any faith, and they are used by Jews, Muslims, Sikhs, Buddhists, Hindus and secular individuals and schools.

By applying these principles with your children, you can go far beyond simply teaching them the tenets of your faith or even an understanding of its scriptures. You can provide an environment that will nurture a personal experience for your child with his own inner life.

8

Learning about God
Ages 6 to 12

A five-year-old asked his mother, "Who do you love more, me or God?"

When she replied that she loved him more, he answered her, "I think this is your big mistake."

Even at this young age, he understood that God should be the first love in all of our lives.

Around the age of 6 or 7, your child will enter a period of transformation, moving from the absorbent mind of early childhood to the reasoning mind. Some children begin this transformation somewhat earlier, at about 5, and some closer to 8. You will notice the change from one period to another when the child moves from asking "what" to asking "why." Baby teeth begin to fall out, the child often loses his baby fat and he enters a new arena of life more independent from his parents and less closely attached to them. In addition to these physical changes, there is a profound change in the way the mind works.

The reasoning mind

The reasoning mind is the mind we have as adults. With this new type of mind come great powers of imagination, abstract thought and the ability to analyze and research. Children now begin to engage in conscious learning and memorization.

The period from 6 to 12 years is the time when children can learn incredible quantities of information. Montessori notes that they are at their academic peak in these years of elementary school. Much of the body of facts we recall in our adulthood is based on what we learned in those active years.

These changes in development from the absorbent mind to the reasoning mind are noted the world over, and it is no accident that formal schooling and religious instruction generally begin at age 6. In the matter of schooling this is generally the age for first grade. In the Catholic Church, for example, this is the age of instruction for First Holy Communion, the first formal instruction in the tenets of faith.

In many traditions, rites of passage for young boys and girls take place at the end of this period. In Christian Confirmation and the Bar Mitzvah of Judaism, the child's formal knowledge of his faith is tested, and having passed this test, the mantle of adulthood in the faith is bestowed by elders and accepted by the youth.

The elementary years are the prime time for learning about one's religion and spiritual beliefs. Even as we take advantage of the ability of children in these years to learn the laws and history of our people or our religion, we never want to lose sight of the inner experience. For spirituality to be meaningful for children of this age, it must not become a rote experience.

The elementary years are a time when most children love to learn. They have not yet grown into adolescence, when their interests and attitudes may change and their innate capacity for academic learning diminishes.

Children are thrilled to learn about anything and everything we can manage to introduce to them *if* we can present it in a way that captures their interest. The question of whether a parent or teacher presents material in a way that elicits interest is a big "if." My own boredom in elementary school in comparison to the excitement I saw every day in the Montessori classrooms I taught is an example of how different life can be for your child when material is made interesting. Montessori explains how we can make things interesting:

> The secret of good teaching is to regard the child's intelligence as a fertile field in which seeds may be sown to grow under the heat of the flaming imagination. Our aim therefore is not merely to make the child understand, and still less to force him to memorize, but to so touch his imagination as to enthuse him to his inmost core.[1]

How we do that is one of Maria Montessori's most valued contributions.

The Cosmic Plan

For this age group, Montessori developed what she called the "cosmic plan." This is a way of teaching that begins with a study of the universe, stories of creation and the development of life on earth. Every subject is taught within this context, and children see that everything is fundamentally intertwined and there is a framework for all knowledge.

I recall being so utterly bored in elementary school because there didn't seem to be any purpose in what we were doing. We moved from one textbook to the next like clockwork (actually, it was not only *like* clockwork, it *was* clockwork), with no relationships between subjects at all.

If we teach by introducing broad topics with stories and charts to give an overview and if children are permitted to choose which topics capture their interest as the way to approach a specific subject, children find that learning can be fascinating, and the results are astounding. We discover two important things about teaching secular or sacred material to children.

- To teach details brings confusion; to establish the relationship between things brings knowledge.
- There is a mental independence that emerges quite naturally during this period, and while we may determine the scope of what we will teach, the child's interests may guide us in selecting where to begin.

In my teaching career, I have found that once you help children find a point of entry to a subject that captures their interest, they have an almost endless desire for more and deeper knowledge. I have seen hundreds of children who love coming to school and who even beg to come on Saturdays because there are so many interesting things to do in class. Children in spiritual development classes that truly meet their needs likewise often beg to come more often.

The spirits of these children are open to life. We undertake to meet their needs for knowledge and wisdom, for awe and wonder. Montessori wrote that mental growth and emotional growth are linked, and therefore learning should be built on a foundation of love of the subject. "Once this love is kindled, all problems confronting the educator will disappear."[2] As the great Italian poet Dante wrote, "The greatest wisdom is first to love."

The True Vine

How do we enthuse the child for his own inner life and help him feel connected to it? Once again we may turn to parable.

For this age group, especially children 6 to 8 years old, Cavalletti's experiences led her to identify the parable of the True Vine, from John 15, verses 1–11, as a key connection with the inner life. This is a complex parable, and it may be read and understood at many levels. However, it is all too easy for adults to underestimate what children can actually grasp and understand. The image of connection of the vine with its branches and fruit is a powerful metaphor for connection with the spirit, no matter what your beliefs.

I am the true vine, and my Father is the husbandman. Every branch in me that beareth not fruit he taketh away: and every branch that beareth fruit, he purgeth it, that it may bring forth more fruit.

Now ye are clean through the word which I have spoken unto you. Abide in me, and I in you. As the branch cannot bear fruit of itself, except it abide in the vine; no more can ye, except ye abide in me.

I am the vine, ye are the branches: He that abideth in me, and I in him, the same bringeth forth much fruit: for without me ye can do nothing. If a man abide not in me, he is cast forth as a branch, and is withered; and men gather them, and cast them into the fire, and they are burned. If ye abide in me, and my words abide in you, ye shall ask what ye will, and it shall be done unto you.

Herein is my Father glorified, that ye bear much fruit; so shall ye be my disciples. As the Father hath loved me, so have I loved you: continue ye in my love. If ye keep my commandments, ye shall abide in my love; even as I have kept my Father's commandments, and abide in his love.

These things have I spoken unto you, that my joy might remain in you, and that your joy might be full.

This parable is introduced with an overview of the idea of unity with the spirit. The sap in the vine is as important to the plants as our blood is to our bodies. There may be blocks to the flow, but they can be overcome. It is a very mystical and yet comforting parable.

After the initial story and discussion, we read the actual parable from the Bible, with a lit candle to represent the sacredness of scripture. Following the reading, you may show a photograph or a model of a vine and its branches. At the elementary level movable material is no longer such a necessity as it was with the younger children.

Discuss the fact that each branch is different. Some are large and some are small. Some are fruitful and some are barren. Some are beautiful and some are very simple. Allow the children to consider the parallels between the vine and its sap and themselves and the spirit.

Help the children also discover the similarities between these two ways Jesus described himself—as a shepherd, the Good Shepherd and as a vine, the True Vine.

As with the parable of the Good Shepherd, provide the source material to the children and ask questions, but don't provide answers or conclusions. The aim is for them to have a personal experience of this relationship at the level of the heart.

Moral development

Moral development also begins in earnest during this period, as the child begins to judge and evaluate all she sees. Her sense of justice becomes pronounced. Parents notice that children begin to complain that "so and so did this to me." Adults may dismiss it as tattling, but this propensity exists because the child is trying to find out from you, the authority, what is okay and what is not.

Children are watching and learning about what is right and wrong from other children and from their parents. In this period the child is ready to learn to think for himself, which is a natural offshoot of the reasoning mind. We must teach him the values we hold dear so that he can use those values to determine the rightness and wrongness of the things going on in his life. If we try to do this for him, we may leave him crippled, unable to act without someone telling him what to do.

By the time your child has entered the reasoning mind he has hopefully already developed an inclination toward the inner life of the spirit. The love and reassurance that were provided in the early years are the foundation for the moral stage newly developing.

Maxims

To help children make sound value judgments, you can teach them simple, straightforward maxims. You can take these from scriptures or from other rich sources, such as the writings of Benjamin Franklin or Hawkins' rules, which George Washington lived by as a child.[3]

When you select the maxims you want to introduce, write them or print them. You can mount them on marble-like contact paper or whatever background you think will be most appealing to your child. When we teach them, it is best to frame them in terms of what you "can" do, rather than what you "must" do.

Here are some examples:

- Love thy neighbor as thyself. *Mark 12:31*
- Ask and you shall receive. Seek and you will find. Knock and the door shall be opened. *Matthew 7:7*
- I say do not forgive seven times, but seventy times seven. *Matthew 18:21*
- Resolve to perform what you ought. Perform without fail what you resolve. *Poor Richard's Almanack*
- Every action done in company ought to be with some sign of respect to those that are present. *"Rules of Civility & Decent Behaviour in Company and Conversation," by George Washington*

Setting standards

Every family has standards, whether they are spoken or unspoken. It is helpful for parents to discuss these standards and to make them clear and consistent to their children. The maxims that you select can be a living part of this. Unfortunately, many parents set arbitrary boundaries when they are tired or upset. I know I've done it. The next day, when the parent is feeling better, the rules are different. This is confusing for children and causes them to continue to push to discover where the boundaries really are. Consistency may sometimes be difficult in the moment, but in the long run it is easier for everyone.

It is very valuable for parents to spend time together discussing the rules and standards of the household so they can stand together in upholding them. One of the more difficult situations in families is when one parent says something is okay and the other parent says absolutely not. If you find yourself in such a situation, it is worth putting off a decision for a few hours so you can consult and mutually agree upon a decision. Standards are the expression of your values. Your values are the foundations of daily decision making. Your children will be observing you day in and day out. When your actions match your stated values, there is an integrity that your child will internalize.

Sometimes, however, we are not perfect! I recall an unfortunate moment in my own life when I heard my father talking about something he had done which was not honest. The image of my father as my hero and the most brilliant and perfect man was a bit tarnished that day. I was only 10, but I still remember the shock of it. It would have been such a relief to me if he had said that he made a mistake and explained what he learned from it rather than boasting about it.

As both a parent and a teacher, I have learned that not knowing an answer is alright. In fact, it can be fun to admit to your child that you don't know and the two of you can find out together. Or in situations where you lose your temper or do something in the presence of your child that you later regret, try letting your child know that you are sorry for what you did. Perhaps share what you will do to make restitution if necessary. I sometimes think *Pride and Prejudice* could be rewritten as a story between parents and children when I see a parent stubbornly unable to admit a momentary lapse or even repeated mistakes to his child.

The more clearly you can articulate and live your values, the more likely it is that your children will respect them and internalize the values themselves. Set the standards high enough so that you enjoy living in your own home. I have been in homes where the children ruled the roost and the parents were in near despair at their inability to ever control them. The family I observed in the restaurant at Disney World may have been suffering under such a situation.

If you live in such a house, find the determination that you will regain control, in a loving but firm way. Children want and need their parents to be in charge; but human nature being what it is, most children will take advantage of perceived weakness and push the boundaries relentlessly.

Much of the mass media that our children are exposed to is not serving the inner life of the child. So don't be afraid to say yes to some programs and no to others. We would go to almost any lengths to defend the physical lives of our children. But somehow, we are not always aware of how devastating the incessant bombarding of sounds and images of twenty-first century media may be upon their inner lives and spirituality. We do not always understand that their sweet innocence may need our vigorous defense as well.

If you have a television in your home, you will have to decide what and how much is acceptable. It is a very good idea to watch television shows and movies and play video games with your children before they are allowed to watch or play them independently. Parental controls on televisions and computers can help, but personal awareness of what children are taking in is also important. Predators of all kinds—from sexual to financial—may exist behind the scenes. They can far too easily worm their way into your child's inner life if you are not alert.

Sometimes we have to gradually wean our children away from things that are not good for them, such as too much television or video gaming. There is beauty in our world and learning to look for it and acknowledge it nurtures the spirit. One way to look at it is that every hour your child spends in front of an electronic screen is an hour not spent playing, being outside or being in connection with his inner life.

Try a day or a week or a month without television or iPods or video games. Spend more time in nature and encourage your child to play outside. Do some star-gazing. Encourage the natural philosopher in your child to express itself. Feed your child's curiosity as soon as it emerges by a visit to the library, a field trip or an online search to follow the threads of new interests. When you nurture and encourage your child's interests and find creative ways to support them, you just may be helping your child find his or her passion.

Exploring the wider world

During the elementary years, one of the developmental tasks for the child is to learn about the culture in which he lives. His sphere of awareness now extends beyond the family to the larger world.

This is an important time for the child to go out of the home, out of the classroom and into marketplaces and work-places for guided experiences in the broader world. If a child is interested in animals, visit a veterinarian. If he thinks being a politician would be great, visit your local congressman.

Children need to be in touch with real possibilities for their own lives. I so often think back to the class of children I described in Chapter 4 and how a year of nurturing helped them become more aware of their own potential. One child in particular became vitally interested in numbers and mathematics in third grade. He is now in college as a math major. Hobbies that develop at this age because of special interests may develop into passions and even into productive careers.

It is always a good idea to encourage hobbies and special field trips for other reasons as well. Every young child loves to spend special time with mom or dad, and if it takes him to new places he is vitally interested in, so much the better. As my own children grew, I always made sure I took each child out for lunch, for some shopping, or to a special art exhibit or sports activity every month or so. Sometimes I found one of my children warming to a subject he or she would never have thought about had I not introduced it in one of our outings.

All too soon the culture of adolescence will try to rob your child of his native interests and soul qualities, and unfortunately not all school settings are conducive to children expressing their own individual interests. The more you can help your child develop momentums in his earlier years of honoring and following his own interests, of learning and making good decisions, the stronger he will be in the face of the influence of peers and the mass-media culture.

We know the teen years can be trying beyond words. The stronger a child is before going into them, the better he will navigate through them. For many families the struggle is literally to keep their children alive. Drugs, alcohol and early sex have become so woven into our youth culture that making choices not to indulge in them is increasingly difficult. Children need not only their parents to love them no matter what, but they also need their own inner strength, mentors and peer groups that support their decisions.

Preparing for the tests of the teen years

An important part of the preparation for the challenges of the teenage years is building a strong foundation in the inner life. There are many components of this inner life, based on what the child has been taught and his own direct spiritual experiences. Giving children a foundation in the beliefs that we follow does not mean we require that our children choose the same path in adulthood. Ultimately it is out of our control. Yet what we pass on to them should include a sound understanding of our own spiritual beliefs and how those beliefs translate into daily life choices.

Most important is that we model the path of our beliefs as we understand it. In the business world it is called "walking the talk." We can also teach it as thoroughly and as well as we can. Then we look to and trust the spirit within the child for the increase in her spiritual development.

If you are part of an established religion or spiritual tradition or path, explore what materials, activities and programs are available for your child. Children from six to twelve are in a time of development when they form relationships outside the family and generally enjoy group activities. If your church or spiritual organization has Sunday school or other group activities available, you may wish to explore them with your child. When children form strong bonds in elementary youth groups, many evolve into viable, supportive teen groups.

If supportive group activities do not exist in your area, consider working with other parents to start a program. Ready-to-use educational materials are available from a number of different sources, or you may wish to create your own program based on books, stories and ideas you would enjoy teaching to your child. See the Resources section at the end of this book for a few recommended sources. You will find many other resources at your local public library and on the Internet.

Look for teachable moments

One of the best ways to impart the teachings and values you treasure is to help your child see the spiritual perspective on the events in her life and in your family affairs. In other words, take advantage of teachable moments.

Children are most impressionable and open to learning when something affects them personally and emotionally. Use moments such as the death of a pet or the moving away of a best friend to talk to your children about the continuity of life and God's comfort to those who mourn. If someone has hurt them, use this as an opportunity to talk about forgiveness and compassion, as in the story of Josh in Chapter 5. When they are happy and feel good about life, reflect on how blessed you are, in so many ways. One gem of truth that comes at just the right time will likely remain and grow in your child more than fifty platitudes you had her memorize.

Find a regular time every day when you talk and share with your child. Some families devote dinner time to family discussions. Some parents find that a few minutes after school or before bedtime work best.

Keep the communication lines open, even when it is difficult to hear what your child has to say. You may be shocked to hear what goes on among younger and younger children and teens today, but if you can suspend judgment and simply listen, your child will be more likely to share again and again. Allow her to share her feelings with you. Try to keep your part of the conversation positive and uplifting but authentic, even when you have to take some form of disciplinary action based on what your child tells you.

It is important that our children learn that they can trust us with anything. They can tell us their deepest, darkest secrets and we will still love them. The seeds of trust you sow with your children early in life can sustain rich relationships throughout life.

Get involved in the life of your child. Get to know your child's friends and what is happening in school and on the playgrounds. Support your child's interests by initiating conversations, planning activities together, chaperoning field trips and visiting the library to find more about special interests. Know the books and movies and music your child likes. Watch movies together and discuss the kinds of decisions and actions the characters are making. When your family is planning a vacation, include the children in planning the itinerary when possible.

Talking with children consistently at an early age with openness and sensitivity helps to build strong bridges so they are less likely to create walls around themselves when they are teenagers. Building a relationship with children in their early years lays a spiritual foundation that will support them well through the challenging teenage years.

Your continuing role

Parents have a pivotal role to play in these elementary years in continuing the spiritual education of their children. Even if there are wonderful programs of spiritual instruction in your child's school or church, his spiritual growth will benefit immensely if spiritual teaching also continues at home. The larger lesson is that spirituality is not just something that we pursue on Sunday and forget the rest of the week, but something valuable that we integrate into our lives.

The idea is to make spiritual learning so interesting that it resonates with the child's inner being and integrates into daily life. Whether it be music, art, science, activities or pets, try to help your child pursue and develop his interests and talents.

You may be thinking to yourself that your child is far more interested in television and Xbox games than in the inner life. That may be true most of the time. We do not expect children to spend all their free time meditating and praying.

However, every child has an inner life, and what we can do is provide the environment and the encouragement for that inner life and the values associated with it to be a living part of our child's outer life.

In short, we can help our children achieve integration.

9

Building Virtues
Activities and Lessons
for Ages 6 to 12

The Story of Cece

From the memoirs of Sr. Maria Antonia

Cece was a little girl growing up in Brazil. She had many spiritual experiences that changed her life. One of her hardest lessons was when her father bought her a wonderful toy car with a little girl inside and a flock of geese following it. When she pulled the string to make the car go, the little girl clapped her hands and the geese flapped their wings. It was a wonderful toy, and she loved it more than all of her other toys.

A very poor little boy used to watch her go by with her toy. You could tell by looking at him that he wanted it. One day he asked her if she would trade her toy car for an orange. Cece said proudly, "My car is worth more than an entire sack of oranges. And besides, I already have all the oranges I want!"

As soon as the words came out, Cece felt the hand of what she believed to be her guardian angel on her head, and she heard him speaking to her. He told her to give the car to the little boy.

Her first thought was, "I can't, I won't—my father gave it to me!" She did not want to give up her toy! But she felt she could not ignore the voice of her guardian angel.

She gave the car to the little boy and took the orange, and she immediately saw the face of her guardian angel fill with sweetness. She knew she had pleased he whom she called the Good God. She felt happier than she had ever felt before, and the orange was especially sweet.

An important factor in the child's spiritual development is the formation of moral values, which occurs in earnest during the elementary years based on the love and security established in the earliest years. The setting of standards within our families creates the foundation for moral values and a strong character. Building a framework of specific virtues is one important aspect of character development during childhood, and using virtues as a focus can help create a strong platform for successfully navigating the challenges of life.

Building virtue

It is not enough to stop negative behaviors in our children; we want to help our children build positive qualities. One successful and fun way to help our children build characters of virtue is by making virtues a focus of our time spent together. The lessons of learning to replace negative thoughts and desires with virtuous qualities begin in early childhood, but they do not end there. They continue through the elementary and teen years and on into adulthood.

Every day of our lives we make choices, both major and minor, whether to do the right thing or not, whether to listen to the voice of conscience or to compromise our values. The choices may become more subtle or complex as we get older, but they never go away!

Many wondrous virtues are just waiting to be expressed. How can we systematically call the attention of our children to these virtues and cultivate them in daily life? Family time framed around stories and discussion about virtues is an effective way to begin this process. Maria Montessori wrote that it is more effective to show the right way to do things rather than to correct the wrong way. Stories are a powerful way to illustrate the right ways to handle situations and what happens as the result of choices, good or bad.

The great sages and saints have taught us much about virtue. The Bible, other religious texts and the great literature of the world are full of inspirational stories of souls meeting the challenges of life with victories, both large and small. Not all the stories are about children, but each tells the tale of the testing of virtue. They are inspiring and filled with honor.

Children need repeated examples and clear choices to help them develop conscience, inner standards and spiritual habits in order to make positive choices. Embedding the examples of virtue and honor in stories makes learning interesting, enjoyable and relevant. Reading and reflecting on these stories also provides opportunities for you to share and to pass on to your children what is most important in your own inner life.

A clock of virtues

Several years ago I worked with a colleague on a project to compile a list of virtues and selected stories to illustrate each virtue. Since we had twelve virtues, we used the hours of the clock to organize these virtues and the corresponding stories so they can be studied in a systematic way. Since there are twelve lines of the clock, parents can choose one virtue per month to read about and discuss with their children.

We drew our stories from three classic anthologies that are readily available at local libraries and bookstores:

- *The Children's Book of Virtues*, by William Bennett
- *The Children's Book of Home and Family*, by William Bennett
- *Family Faith Treasury*, by Eva Moore

We chose stories from these collections for the virtues they embody and placed them on the lines of our clock. These stories help children become aware that around the world young people in the past have faced similar challenges to the ones they face today, and in every culture parents strive to teach their children kindness, helpfulness and wisdom. Many of the stories are thrilling tales of challenges faced and conquered.

The table on the following pages lists the twelve virtues, corresponding qualities, and stories from the resource books listed above (titles are indicated by their initials). Once you begin to work with the theme of each virtue, you may want to add your own favorite stories or write your own.

A Clock of Virtues

12 o'clock • Power
responsible
hardworking
ability to lead
ability to develop
  and follow a plan

"Over in the Meadow" *CBV*
"Teddy Roosevelt: Family Man" *CBH*
"The Story of Moses" *FFT*
"Abraham, Father of a Nation" *FFT*

1 o'clock • Love
kind
friendly
cheerful
merciful
forgiving
loving freedom

"Legend of the Dipper" *CBV*
"Sermon to the Birds" *CBV*
"Kindness to Animals" *CBV*
"Elizabeth's Roses" *CBH*
"The Good Shepherd" *FFT*
"The Real Neighbor" *FFT*

2 o'clock • Mastery
spiritual
devoted
compassionate
peaceful
courageous
masterful

"The Stars in the Sky" *CBV*
"The Story of William Tell" *FFT*
"Aesop's The Wind and the Sun" *FFT*

3 o'clock • Control
self-control
humility
faith
patience

"The King and His Hawk" *CBV*
"The Little Red Hen" *CBV*
"Penelope's Web" *CBH*
"Jesus is Born" *FFT*

4 o'clock • Obedience
determined
trustworthy
loyal
obedient to the
  voice of
  conscience

"Saint George and the Dragon" *CBV*
"The Old Fox" *FFT*

5 o'clock • Wisdom
intuitive
wise
understanding
thirsting for
  knowledge
creating unity
  through
  communication
solving problems

"The Honest Woodsman" *CBV*
"Hercules and the Wagoner" *CBV*
"Cornelia's Jewels" *CBH*
"Ladders to Heaven—A Legend" *FFT*
"Jesus the Teacher" *FFT*

A Clock of Virtues (cont'd)

6 o'clock • Harmony

orderly   "Louisa May Alcott's Dream" *CBH*
cooperative   "Jane Addams and the Hull House" *CBH*
team worker   "A Story about a Farmer" *FFT*
peace-maker
harmonious family
   member

7 o'clock • Gratitude

generous   "Ruth and Naomi" *CBH*
magnanimous   "Aesop's The Lion and the Mouse" *FFT*
friendly   "The Birds' Gifts: A Ukrainian
polite   Easter Story" *FFT*
grateful
sensitive

8 o'clock • Justice

service   "What Bradley Owed" *CBH*
fairness   "Aesop's The Hares and the Frogs" *FFT*
tolerance   "Jonah and the Big Fish" *FFT*
discipline   "The Story of Two Sons" *FFT*
citizenship

9 o'clock • Reality

responsible   "Aesop's The Boy Who Cried 'Wolf'" *CBV*
honest   "Abe Speaks Out" *FFT*
peaceful   "Aesop's The Thirsty Crow" *FFT*
hardworking   "Aesop's The Fox and the Mask" *FFT*
feeling at home   "Aesop's The Jay and the Peacocks" *FFT*
   in the universe

10 o'clock • Vision

generosity   "George Washington and
unselfishness   His Cherry Tree" *CBV*
concentration   "The Place of Brotherhood" *CBH*
ability to follow   "Johnny Appleseed and
   through   the Pioneers" *FFT*
truthfulness   "Jesus Feeds Five Thousand" *FFT*

11 o'clock • Victory

independent   "The Little Hero of Holland" *CBV*
dependable   "The Wright Brothers" *CBH*
spiritual   "Into the Promised Land" *FFT*
joyful   "Aesop's The Ant and
striving for   the Grasshopper" *FFT*
   excellence

In order to create a balanced personality in children, it is important to help them to develop a wide array of virtues. We all have natural strengths in one or more areas, and so do our children. We naturally want to encourage them. Even so, we can also encourage them to develop broadly in many areas, as weakness in one area can impede the full expression of virtue in another.

Take for instance a person who has tremendous strength in leadership abilities. If this gift is not tempered with love and wisdom, the person may become a tyrant. On the other hand, you may have someone with great creative, imaginative abilities, but if that individual cannot harness that ability with practical self-discipline, the wonders of his artistic vision may remain unexpressed and his potential unfulfilled.

Through loving family relationships and open, encouraging discussions, your children have a greater opportunity to integrate their virtue lessons in personal ways. Set aside a regular family time to read about and reflect on the virtues. This should be a time when the interruptions and problems of life are held at bay so you can commune together, heart to heart.

A scheduled family get-together may seem foreign at first, but give it a try and let it unfold according to the uniqueness of your family. You may find it becomes a highlight of family life that no one wants to miss. Older children can make snacks for the family and even read the stories sometimes. Parents as well as children can share (when appropriate) their personal challenges in living the virtues.

Some families like to focus on one virtue a month going in the order we listed. Others pick whatever is relevant to family members. Some families meet two or three times on one virtue, while others plan one meeting per virtue. Some parents prefer just to read the stories and see what comes of them.

There is no right or wrong way to do this, so jump in, experiment, and make it your own. The very act of making a commitment to the growth of virtues will strengthen the fabric of your family's life. You may find that this exercise strengthens your own inner life as much as that of your children.

The Golden Rule

The period from 6 to 12 years of age is a wonderful period to explore the Golden Rule: "Do unto others as you would have others do unto you."

We find the Golden Rule in the scriptures of every major world religion, both in the West and in the East and even in early classical writings. This precept has been expressed in very similar terms for thousands of years.

The Golden Rule is a statement of compassion for others. It leads to actions that are not only good for others but also good for ourselves. It provides us with a simple rule of behavior that encourages us to open our hearts and act with compassion toward our fellow man, thereby being true to our inner selves. Here is how the Golden Rule is expressed in different world religions:

Christianity: Whatsoever ye would that men should do unto you, do ye even so unto them.   —*Jesus, Matt. 7:12*

Judaism: What is hateful to you; do not to your fellow man. This is the law: all the rest is commentary.
—*Hillel, Talmud, Shabbat 31a*

Buddhism: Hurt not others with that which pains thyself.
—*Gautama Buddha, fifth century* B.C.

Hinduism: Do naught to others which if done to thee would cause thee pain.   —*Mahabharata*

Confucianism: Try your best to treat others as you would wish to be treated yourself, and you will find that this is the shortest way to benevolence.   —*Mencius VII.A.4*

Islam: Not one of you is a believer until he loves for his brother what he loves for himself.

—*40 Hadith of an-Nawawi 13*

Ancient Greece: May I do unto others as I would that they should do unto me.   —*Plato, fourth century* B.C.

Shintoism: The heart of the person before you is a mirror. See there your own form.   —*Ko-ji-ki Hachiman Kasuga*

Taoism: Regard your neighbor's gain as your own gain and your neighbor's loss as your own loss.

—*T'ai Shang Kan Ying P'ien*

Jainism: A man should wander about treating all creatures as he himself would be treated.   —*Sutrakritanga 1.11.33*

Sikhism: Treat others as thou wouldst be treated by thyself.
—*Adi Grandth, sixteenth century* A.D.

Zoroastrianism: Do not unto others all that which is not well for oneself.   —*Zoroaster, fifth century* B.C.

Native American lore: All things are our relatives; what we do to everything, we do to ourselves. All is really One.
—*Black Elk, Oglala Lakota 1863–1950*

Ancient Egypt: Do for one who may do for you, that you
may cause him thus to do.
        —*The Tale of the Eloquent Peasant, 1670–1640 B.C.*

This last text, from ancient Egypt, may be the oldest recorded version of this principle.

The simple but powerful teaching of the Golden Rule, stated in so many different ways, clearly permeates the religious and spiritual teachings of the world. It is often considered the most concise and universal principle of ethical behavior. It helps children gain a very basic sense that all peoples strive to be good.

I have taught this several ways in secular schools. I always develop the rules of behavior for my classes with the students through discussions about what we would all like to see. Towards the conclusion of these discussions, I mention there is one rule that is called the Golden Rule.

I talk with them about the value of gold: Why do we love gold so much? It is highly valued throughout the world and has been so honored for many centuries. People refer to the "gold standard" in any business and profession as the best of the best. The color of yellow-gold is often associated with spiritual wisdom. Gold itself is associated with the sun and could even be considered as materialized sunlight.

But there is something even more valuable than gold itself. People all around the world have believed that the most valuable thing in life is kindness to one another. And this is what we mean by the Golden Rule.

I have a stack of cards, each one stating the Golden Rule in the words of a different world religion. I read one per day. When we have gone through all of them, I put them in a little basket for the children to pick them out and read them when they are interested.

Some children use them as the initial step to find out about religions and religious festivals around the world. There are some lovely children's books that show the main features and festivals of each religion. One of my favorites is *The Kid's Book of World Religions,* by Jennifer Glossop.

The Golden Rule is a wonderful thing to teach our children. It is suitable for use in any setting, including secular ones, because the principle is so universal. In your home or in a religious setting, you can extend the discussion with the parable of the Good Samaritan and other teachings that bring home the same message. When you see a real-life example, a newspaper or a magazine article that features someone acting on behalf of others, you can use it as dinner table conversation so the children see the relevance of these teachings in our lives today. My own children and the children with whom I have shared it have often been amazed and delighted to hear that children in other lands and in other religions learn the very same principle.

The inner light

The world's major religions all teach that we have the spirit of the divine inside of us. This seed of spirit may grow and flourish from childhood into adulthood if it is nurtured and encouraged to express itself. Maria Montessori's idea of the child as a "spiritual embryo" emphasized her belief that humans are not merely biological beings, but also spiritual beings seeking expression inside a physical body. This concept of the spiritual embryo is truly humankind's most precious treasure because it is precisely this inherent power that can transform the world as we know it.

Like the Golden Rule, this is a concept that is found in many of the world's religions. You may wish to teach the following concepts to your child to show how this common thread of our innate connection to God is expressed in different ways in the different religious traditions of the world.

The Bible tells us that we are created in the image of God.

Jesus said: "The kingdom of God is within you."
                                                    —*Luke 17:21*

The apostle Paul wrote to the Corinthians: "Know ye not
    that ye are the temple of God, and [that] the Spirit of
    God dwelleth in you?"   —*1 Corinthians 3:16*

Hindu scripture speaks of the light of the Spirit that lives in
    the heart.

Jewish teachings say that there is a divine spark inside of us
    that is like a bridge to heaven.

Buddhists speak of the "germ of Buddhahood," meaning that
    the seed of light in each heart can grow and become a
    Buddha.

According to the teachings of Islam, when God created man,
    he breathed his own spirit into his creation.

In Zoroastrianism, physical fire is revered as a visible symbol
    of the Inner Light, the divine spark that burns in each and
    every heart.

This concept complements the principle of the Golden Rule. If we understand that each soul has the divine spark within, we will treat each person with love and compassion. We are more motivated to help our children connect with the richness of the inner life.

There is a lovely book about Francis of Assisi called *Francis: The Journey and the Dream*. One section tells the story of how Francis made his first connection to the inner light:

> He began to hear a voice inside himself, a deeper, clearer voice that was like discovering a part of himself he did not know was there. The more he prayed ... the deeper he plunged toward some inner force that gave him strength and peace.[1]

The concept of the inner light helps us to transcend division, prejudice and separation between people. If we are all children of God, we are all brothers and sisters.

Guided meditation

Children enjoy guided meditations. It is generally easy for them to visualize what you describe, and when they are in a receptive mood, they may remain fully attentive for many minutes. If you wish to try this particular meditation, which I have given with many delighted children, give your child some basic instruction and then lead her through the beautiful visualizations it contains.

As you slowly and carefully read this meditation aloud, use a soft and gentle voice. You may choose to play classical music at a low volume in the background to help calm and relax your child. The largo movements of symphonies are particularly soothing. I especially like the largo movement of Bach's Double Violin Concerto in D Minor.

Children enjoy props that help them fully engage. As part of your introduction, you might begin with pictures of tropical islands and real or costume jewels for them to examine and handle.

Meditation journey

We are going to imagine we are going to visit an imaginary island in your heart. Here is a picture of a beautiful island to help you get in the mood.

Your island is going to be made of crystals, like these:

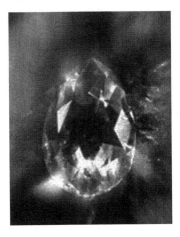

If you have some real jewels or crystals, allow your child to see and handle them. Once they have seen the images or physical items, collect them so they will not be distractions, and ask the children to close their eyes and see with their inner eye what you are going to describe.

Let's get comfortable and take a few deep breaths.

We are going to go into our hearts. Close your eyes and imagine a lovely light blazing in your heart. It is a beautiful flame-spark of God that contains the love, the wisdom and the power of God.

See an island in the midst of a shimmering blue sea inside of your heart. The island is shining with crystals. Instead of the ground we usually see, the island is covered in brilliant green emeralds, clear diamonds of white and yellow, blue sapphires and red rubies. You can smell heavenly scents from flowering trees.

You are arriving at this island and beginning to walk on the sand. You can see the pink sand and hear it crunching beneath your feet. You can hear the soft sound of the waves upon the shore. The sun is warm on your shoulders as you walk into the lush tropical trees and flowers of many delicate colors. The flowers smell like roses and carnations. Colorful birds perch on the branches of the trees. They are singing songs you have never heard before—songs of heaven that make your spirit sing.

As you walk onto the island you see a hill ahead that leads to the center of the island. You feel surrounded by love and comfort as you walk toward the hill.

At the top of the hill you see a platform and a beautifully carved gold, jeweled throne. A soft velvet cushion rests upon the

throne. You see the blue sky and the trees in the background.
As we see this beauteous throne, we pray:
[Feel free to change these words to fit your beliefs.]

O Lord my God,
Come and walk and talk with me
In this my paradise garden
My island in the sea!

Our Lord, the living One, comes to sit upon the throne.
Feel the love of God fill your entire being as you see him there,
at home in your own heart.

Allow your child to remain in the meditation as long as she is still and engaged. When you see her move or open her eyes, it is time to close your session. She may want to talk about it or she may not. To extend the experience and take it to another level, ask your child if she would like to make a drawing or a painting of her island in the sea.

Remember, where your attention goes, your energy flows. Meditations like this are powerful ways to create a focus on spirit.

Maps

Children learn by doing, especially in the early years of this period. You could take the previous meditation on the island in the heart and your child could make a salt-dough island decorated with sequins or faux jewels you can get at any craft store. (Salt dough is a thick dough made from salt and flour. Recipes and instructions for making it are easily found on the Internet.)

A salt-dough map of the Holy Land. The star shows where Jesus was born and the cross shows where he was crucified.

If you are studying Bible geography and the Holy Land or a specific historical figure from ancient times, get a large map and track the movements of the people in your study. For example, you could trace on the map the journey of the Israelites from Egypt to the Holy Land, Jesus' travels as he taught, or the travels of an explorer whose courage your child admires. You can track with push pins and yarn or even better, make a three-dimensional salt-dough map.

As children shape with their hands the contours of the map and the topography of mountains, valleys, rivers and seas, they internalize the details of geography much more deeply than they would by just seeing it. Following the footsteps of the master in your chosen religious faith and providing short teachings at each location puts those teachings into the context of real people in real places. It makes the teaching come alive for children, even as they learn about the world.

10

Spiritual Preparation
for Parents and Teachers

On Children

Your children are not your children. They are the
sons and daughters of Life's longing for itself.

They come through you but not from you, and
though they are with you, yet they belong not to you.

You may give them your love but not your
thoughts. For they have their own thoughts.

You may house their bodies but not their souls,
for their souls dwell in the house of tomorrow, which
you cannot visit, not even in your dreams.

You may strive to be like them, but seek not to
make them like you. For life goes not backward nor
tarries with yesterday.

You are the bows from which your children as
living arrows are sent forth. The archer sees the mark
upon the path of the infinite, and He bends you with
His might that His arrows may go swift and far.

Let your bending in the archer's hand be for
gladness; for even as he loves the arrow that flies,
so He loves also the bow that is stable.

—*from* The Prophet

It all starts with you. If you wish to nurture the inner life of your child, it is important that you begin by consciously nurturing your own inner life. Even more than what you teach, it is the spirituality that you live in your own life that will leave a lasting impression on your children.

I love Robin Casarjian's simple suggestion, "Take time to come home to yourself every day." In our busy lives, many of us discover that we are not taking time for ourselves and our own inner lives. Even if it is only a few minutes each day, make the time you need to commune with the inner life of the spirit, to give your daily prayers and devotions, and to find peace within yourself.

Sometimes it is a challenge, especially as a parent, when there are so many demands on our time, but even in the busiest schedule, it is always possible to find some time to direct your thoughts to the realm of spirit. Even while you are functioning in the outer world and fulfilling the tasks at hand, there is a part of you that can maintain that inner tie.

A wonderful example of this is the story of Brother Lawrence, a lay brother who served in the kitchen of a Carmelite monastery in Paris in the seventeenth century. He was known for his ability to always have his mind on God, even in the midst of the busiest outer activities. His words have been collected in the spiritual classic, *The Practice of the Presence of God*. He said:

> The time of business does not differ for me from the time of prayer; and in the noise and clatter of my kitchen, while several persons are at the same time calling for different things, I possess God in as great tranquility as if I were on my knees at the blessed sacrament.[1]

Even so, sometimes it is necessary to stop to smell the proverbial roses. There is a trail in Grand Teton National Park that winds up several miles from a flat, dry field and reaches the most amazing pristine alpine lakes at the base of the Grand Teton Mountain. I hike this trail every year, usually in the glorious Indian summer so common to that region.

Even when I'm not there, I can see in my mind's eye the wildflowers at each turn of the trail. I can see rocky steps in portions of the trail and those spots that are often muddy, and I can see and hear a small waterfall I pass on the trail upward. The waterfall is lovely enough, but it is just the foreground for the mountain far in the distance peeking up just above the falls, like a glistening stone in its perfectly sculpted setting.

Why do I so easily remember these things, even though my last trip was more than six months ago? I feel so vividly alive on that mountain—I'm joyful, energetic, peaceful, competent, clear and happy to be alive. That mountain trail nurtures my spirit, and I love nothing more than to bring my adult children with me so I can nurture their spirits as well.

I cannot hike on my special trail in the Grand Teton Mountains every day, but I can sit and imagine it—or I can

The Grand Teton, Wyoming

go for a walk in a neighboring park and allow myself to blend into nature and experience that aliveness again. I grew up by the beach and the mountains, and both environments bring me to a pristine state of mind. It is difficult to put it into words, but it is almost as though these special places initiate me into a higher, fuller and more joyful state of consciousness. I find I need to renew this energizing experience at intervals in my life.

What works for you to energize your spirit? What works for your children?

For one of my children a garden, especially a garden with many flowers, is like a magical potion. We were traveling one time and the children were at one another's throats. We stopped at a flower extravaganza in St. Louis and within twenty minutes, the harmony was totally restored, and it lasted for the rest of the afternoon. The flowers put the children in contact with their inner spirit and took their attention away from the petty annoyances with each other.

When you are heart-centered and connected with your inner

spirit, your children will see this and they will feel the same. When we as parents are happy, our children are happy, too. And when we are stressed, our children are the first to suffer.

One of my children in particular has always been very perceptive of people's feelings. She walks into a room and immediately knows how her friends and family are feeling. She senses if anyone is down about anything and comes to give us a hug or a kiss. When I see this I can only hope I was half as nurturing as a parent to her as she is nurturing to me as my child.

The role of parents

Many people have turned to their churches to find help in raising their children and teaching them about spirituality. Regardless of what may be available in church, school or the local community, parents have an indispensable role to play in supporting the spiritual growth of the child. In *The Family Friendly Church*, author Ben Freudenburg shares the insights he has gained about what really helps children stay bonded to their families and the values they are raised with.

He found that in the use of drugs, alcohol and sex there was virtually no difference in the statistics of "churched" kids versus "unchurched" kids. You can imagine that for a youth minister this would be very discouraging news. It was for Ben, and so he took a sabbatical to determine why this was so.

His book chronicles the research he did to find some answers. He discovered that there are four things that make the difference to help young people stay on a positive and healthy path. In fact, these simple family practices have proven more effective than many parent and church programs:

1. Talking about faith with your mother
2. Talking about faith with your father
3. Having family devotions or prayer
4. Participation in family projects to help other people[2]

Freudenburg found that his focus as a youth worker had been in the wrong place. Instead of having wonderful programs for children in the church, supported by parents, what children really need is strong families supported by the church. The first place he applied his newfound wisdom was in his own home with his own family.

You, the parents, are your child's first and most important teachers. More than programs, children need you! Whether you are a churchgoer or not, try to live your beliefs and values before your children.

Children will surely do what their parents do more readily than what they are told to do. No matter what the ages of your children, parents remain key role models. Talk with them about your own beliefs and your road in developing or accepting them. Help your children understand why you make the decisions you make and explain the values behind those decisions.

We find ourselves living in a time when the prevailing culture tends largely to deny or ignore the spiritual side of life. Montessori offers an interesting insight into why the spiritual life is not more fully regarded: "Our civilization has not yet devised means of defense for the spirit similar to those devised for the body through hygiene."[3]

This book is an attempt to generate parental thought about this very subject and to suggest practical ways we can nurture and protect the inner life of our children. Our deepest desires to raise up our nations as well as our families are bound up in this process. Montessori wrote in *The Secret of Childhood*: "It is the spirit of the child that can determine the course of human progress and lead it perhaps even to a higher form or civilization."[4]

We cannot expect that our children of any age are going to get the necessary spiritual nurturing from most schools and many aspects of the culture we live in. We can do our best to find schools, churches and other environments outside the home that will support our children's inner life. When you are looking at options for activities your child might participate in—music lessons, sports or any other program—consider the adults who will be supervising or teaching. It is not necessary that they share your beliefs, but it is important that they are competent, kind and able to support the child's spiritual path and values.

But ultimately, it is up to us as parents. We are the ones ultimately responsible for our own children. When we know and understand more, we will find more and better ways to raise our children to be fine, fulfilled human beings.

Blocks to our relationships with children

The great English poet, William Wordsworth wrote these simple words: "The child is the father of the man."[5] He understood that it is during the years of early childhood that the men and women of tomorrow are formed. Children are not just miniature adults. Building the person to be is the work of the child. Understanding the profound importance of the role of childhood in human life is the first step in being able to serve the child.

How do we prompt within ourselves the deep change of heart necessary to accept this understanding? Maria Montessori spoke of it as an initiation:

We insist on the fact that a teacher must prepare himself interiorly by studying himself so that he can tear out his most deeply rooted defects, those in fact which impede his relations with children. In order to discover these subconscious failings, we have need of a special kind of instruction. We must see ourselves as another sees us. This is equivalent to saying that a teacher must be initiated.[6]

The major "defects" that impede our relations with children are two: pride and anger. Pride makes us think that as the adult we know better—without stopping to observe and allow the possibility that the child might be our teacher. He may be showing us what he really needs, or he may be showing us something about ourselves. Anger may be our reaction when the child does not do what we think he or she ought to be doing. Clearly there are times when children are naughty and need to be corrected, but we can do this out of love rather than anger.

Rather than express pride and anger, we can work toward cultivating their opposites: patience and humility. When we are patient we allow our child to complete his action at his own speed rather than becoming annoyed when he makes us wait. When we are patient we see that the child is trying to do something, even very imperfectly, and it may take twenty more times of practice before he gets it right. He may be quite excited that he finished something even though it is not perfect. We demonstrate humility when we recognize that our child's needs are different than our own and he is his own person.

In social relations with other adults, we get feedback if we are being selfish, prideful or angry. But when we are with children, whether at home with them or in school, we are most often behind closed doors. It is part of human nature that a person with undisputed authority who is not subject to criticism or feedback is in danger of becoming a tyrant. This individual may come to see undisputed authority as his right and will regard any offence against that authority as a crime. Unfortunately this scenario happens in homes and classrooms the world over. The statistics of child abuse bear witness to this.

What Maria Montessori helps us to understand is that often the child's cries or disobedience are not naughtiness or rebellion, but a vital defense of his own inner development. For example we see a child whose inner teacher tells him, "Touch to learn," and whose parent says, "Don't touch!" Whose voice does the child follow, his inner voice or the outer authority?

When there is this kind of discrepancy between the inner and the outer voice, the child experiences a conflict. If he follows his inner teacher and proceeds, he may be seen as defiant. If he surrenders, he may miss an important sensitive period. How can we know the difference between the child's genuine need to work and a spark of naughtiness?

Most parents know the look their child gets when they are doing something they know is naughty. Of course we will intervene if we see deliberate naughtiness and we will intervene if there are expressions of unkindness, danger or time restraints that have to be respected.

When we understand more clearly what developmental tasks our child is working on, we can act in harmony with his inner teacher. We remove ourselves as an obstacle and greatly assist the child's development. This does not in any way mean that we should allow the child to become a tyrant and think he can always have his way. It is as much of a disservice to our children to allow them to do whatever they want as it is to prevent them from doing the developmental work they need to do. Children need boundaries in order to feel secure in the world, and we need to respect the roles of parent and child that we have established.

I remember one day when one of my children was angry with me for something I would not let her do and she stood defiantly with her hands on her hips and said, "You're not the boss of me!" She could not have been more than four at the time.

I looked sweetly at her and said, "Oh, but I am. Let's talk about what just happened." If you are the parent, you are indeed the boss—and hopefully a compassionate one.

Learn to observe

Your child is in many ways an adult soul in a child's body. This person who has come to live with you, love you and be loved by you has the right to be treated with dignity, just as you do. It sometimes requires real effort to sustain our harmony and equanimity each day when the baby is crying and children are getting into mischief. Our children's spiritual growth, as well as our own, depends upon these acts of self-control we make to root out pride and anger.

Observation of the child is at the heart of helping us better understand what our children want and need.

Here is a scenario to consider. A mother has two children, Sam and Sara. Sara has been bothering Sam incessantly. This has been going on for days. One day Sam is seated at the kitchen table coloring with his pencils. Sara is bending over Sam. It looks like she is about to grab his pencil, and mom is deciding whether or not to intervene. To intervene or not to

intervene, that is the perennial question!

Mom sees a thoughtful look in Sara's eyes and waits just a moment. Sara sweetly offers to sharpen one of Sam's pencils. Sam smiles and gives her the pencil; Sara sharpens it and returns it. If mom had interrupted, Sara might not have done another nice thing for Sam for days.

Observation takes time and effort. You often have to suspend judgment while you wait to see what is really happening. The simplest, humblest action on the part of your child may be a very special moment of victory. Take the time to notice. Expect the best of your children and let them show it to you.

Observe your child when she is busy with an activity. When she selects an activity for herself, she is engaged. Through this concentration she develops herself. There is an integration of her mind, which is learning about something, her desire, which chose this activity, and her hand, which is doing the chosen work. This is a powerful combination.

Once we have demonstrated a lesson or activity to a child, we can allow the child to repeat the activity to his heart's content. Montessori described the role of the teacher in the words of John the Baptist as he spoke of his relationship with Christ: "He must increase, but I must decrease." The child increases his activity and the inner development that occurs through the activity, while we momentarily disappear from the child's awareness. We may remain in the room, but we do not disturb the child's concentrated effort.

Serving the child

Preparing to teach our children about spirituality is a process whereby we begin to see the child in a new light, and hence also see ourselves in a new light. Whether you are a teacher or a parent teaching your own child, it is helpful to think about the role of the teacher.

Maria Montessori says the teacher is not a *teacher* at all, but a *director* of the child's energies. In *Spontaneous Activity in Education* she wrote about the real purpose of education:

> I believe that the work of the educator consists primarily in protecting the powers [of the developing child] and directing them without disturbing them in their expansion; and in the bringing of man into contact with the spirit which is within him and should operate through him.[7]

Cavelletti recommends that rather than trying to *teach* religion to children, we should *live* it with them. We do not have to be the person with all the answers, but the humble seeker who proposes experiences that will bring each of us closer to the inner life of the spirit.

Let us keep in mind Montessori's definition of education as "help to life." When we serve the child whom we love, how do we do it?

Montessori suggests that the greatest love we can show our children is to help them think and act for themselves. There are many things they cannot do for themselves, so we surely do not abandon them. But as soon as they show a spontaneous interest and ability to perform a new skill, we can allow them to do it. Whether it is buttoning their jacket, pouring a cup of juice, forming their own sentences or spontaneously saying prayers; even if they do it very imperfectly at first, they gain mastery and confidence in their own abilities if we allow them to do it themselves.

When we prepare an environment that engages the child, he begins to work. His periods of concentration increase. It is this simple action that produces calmness and changes the life of the child. Maria Montessori said that when children really begin to work, "It almost seemed as if a road had opened up within their souls that led to all their latent powers, revealing the better part of themselves."[8]

Teach by teaching, not by correcting

Even if it does not come naturally, you can learn to catch your child doing something right instead of focusing on their negative behavior. You can realize that many mistakes the child makes are out of ignorance. So you can show your child how to do something the way it needs to be done.

I can give you my own example. When I was little I often ran through the house and slammed doors. I did not slam the doors out of anger, but just because I was in a hurry or not aware of what I was doing. It became a sore spot because I was chided for it so many times.

When I took Montessori training, one of the first lessons I learned was how to teach a child to open and shut a door quietly. You stand at the door with the child, slowly and carefully show her how the handle works and how we can watch and feel the turning of the knob. Then we walk through and release the knob carefully as we close the door. As the child practices a few times, we make a game of seeing how silently we can close the door.

I have seen that children love this activity. They love the challenge and they seem to enjoy seeing how the knob mechanism works. I was nearly in tears as I did this lesson, realizing that it probably never even occurred to my loving parents that I simply did not know how to close a door quietly or that it might be interesting to learn how to do so.

We do not want to push our children to achieve or expect perfection, but we can expect sincere effort. When your child misbehaves or makes troubling choices, try to clearly explain the consequences. And be sure to separate his behavior from his true essence. We can love them unconditionally, and make sure they know it. Teach your child how to do well and give examples to follow.

Seeing the child who is not yet there

It is a tragedy when parents give up on their children. We have all seen it: parents who are disappointed in their children's achievements, or parents who criticize and condemn them for one reason or another. What a burden for a child when those who love him the most feel he is somehow not good enough, not smart enough or not beautiful enough.

Children will misbehave. Teenagers will push the boundaries and push them again. These actions are normal—they are part of the process of the child growing and forging an identity separate from parents. Children are not born knowing how to live in this world, so we have much to teach them. Mistakes are entirely normal.

Marva Collins is a former Chicago educator who was so successful in her small school that President Ronald Reagan invited her to be his Secretary of Education. She politely declined, explaining that her most important work was in the classroom. I spent a week observing in her school in the early 1990s and learned that she was fond of encouraging her children by telling them, "If you can't make a mistake, you can't make anything!" She is a wise woman.

Even in the midst of the challenges of raising children—especially in the teenage years—we can continue to hold our children in the highest esteem and steadfastly hold the vision of their potential to be. We can learn to envision the integrity and right action of our children, no matter what behavior they temporarily show.

When we do this for our children, we reinforce their true nature and build their self-esteem. This helps them feel good about who they are and what they can do. Our praise of them has to be linked to real accomplishments, however—even baby steps in the right direction—to mean anything to the child.

When children are engaged in poor choices, we need to help them see the consequences of those choices. By this I do not mean the consequence of getting punished, but rather the consequences of where the poor decision can lead them and what other choices they might make next time.

When we do punish our children, we want to make sure that the punishment fits the crime and that it is a learning experience for them. It is about the child learning to be accountable for his actions rather than being sorry he got caught. We teach this sense of responsibility and accountability to our children because we love them and want to help them learn how to make better choices.

Your child will become, in some great measure, what you believe she can become. We all have the potential to manifest the innate genius of our individuality. Most of us need some help and support to bring it forth. If you see your child as competent, as a child of the spirit, she will have the greatest opportunity to become the fullness of her potential, because you are reinforcing its very existence. What greater gift can we give our children than to buoy them up by our love and enable them to fulfill their greatest potential?

Even before the child manifests the qualities that you believe are there, you have to accept that they are there. This is "seeing the child who is not yet there." Instead of focusing on all of the many imperfections, which are surely there, focus on the better nature and skills that your child is trying to manifest. Love is transforming. It is truly the transforming power of the mother and the father to see beauty in their children, even when they show their naughtiness.

The love that wells up within our hearts for our children is like a bridge between where the child is now and where he can be. It is this love that makes up the difference between the shortcomings of children and the possibility of their becoming more. That gap between present imperfections and future attainment is always filled in by the love of the parent's heart.

It is not possible to be a perfect parent—that is not the goal, any more than having a perfect child is our goal. We often hear that we have to work on our marriages to sustain the relationship. So, too, let us work at being better parents.

Whether your children are toddlers, teens or adults, it is never too late to show them your interest and affection. I recently heard a young father offer this advice to other young people considering becoming parents: "The most important thing you can do for your children is to make sure that they know that you love them."

Many of us will find our greatest fulfillment in raising and teaching our children, especially as we nurture their inner lives. Let us walk this path so that we may be able to say, in the words of Maria Montessori: "I have served the spirits of those children, and they have fulfilled their development, and I kept them company in their experiences."[9]

Resources

Spiritual development of children

The Child in the Church, Maria Montessori

The Religious Potential of the Child, Sofia Cavalletti

Listening to God with Children: The Montessori Method Applied to the Catechesis of Children, Gianna Gobbi

Teaching Godly Play: How to Mentor the Spiritual Development of Children, Jerome W. Berryman
A program for spiritual instruction for children in a group setting, based on Montessori principles

A Spiritual Approach to Parenting, Dr. Marilyn Barrick

Stories from the world's religions for children

The Bible Story, ten volumes covering the Old and New Testaments, Arthur S. Maxwell

Prince Siddhartha: The Story of Buddha, Jonathan Landaw and Janet Brooke

Jataka Tales, a series of illustrated children's books based on stories of previous lives of the Buddha

The Story of Sri Krishna for Children, two volumes, Swami Raghaveshananda

A Faith Like Mine, Laura Buller

Books to read with your children

An Angel to Watch Over Me: True Stories of Children's Encounters with Angels, Joan Wester Anderson

What You Can See, You Can Be! David A. Anderson
an illustrated children's book about the power of positive thinking, imaging your perfect opportunity, friends, etc.

The Children's Book of Virtues, William Bennett

The Children's Book of Home and Family, William Bennett

The Chronicles of Narnia series, C. S. Lewis

Family Faith Treasury, Eva Moore

The Little Engine That Could, Watty Piper

The Little Rabbit Who Wanted Red Wings, Carolyn Sherwin Bailey and Jacqueline Rogers

The Little House on the Prairie (series), Laura Ingalls Wilder

Your favorite children's stories!

The Montessori Method

The Secret of Childhood, Maria Montessori

The Absorbent Mind, Maria Montessori

Maria Montessori Her Life and Work, E. M. Standing

Montessori Madness: A Parent to Parent Argument for Montessori Education, Trevor Eissler

Montessori: The Science Behind the Genius, Angeline Lillard

www.ageofmontessori.com offers articles about Montessori education and links to recommended resources.

Webinars at Age of Montessori

Available for free download at www.ageofmontessori.com

Montessori—What it is and Why it Matters to You!
    Trevor Eissler and Mary Ellen Maunz
    A lively discussion about what is wrong in many
    traditional schools and why Montessori succeeds all over
    the world

Help Your Child Access His/Her Inner Teacher
    Mary Ellen Maunz and Valerie McBride
    Learn how to help the children you love connect with
    their very own inner teacher. When children experience
    the connection to the inner teacher and learn to rely on it,
    they learn more and they become calmer and more joyful.

What It Means to Be a Montessori Parent or Teacher
    Mary Ellen Maunz and Tani Kingston
    Whether you are a teacher or parent, there are simple
    steps you can take now to help unfold a child's
    individuality with confidence and love. This webinar
    explores techniques for successfully interacting with
    children and promoting the harmonious development of
    each child's full potential.

The Universal Needs of Children
    Mary Ellen Maunz and Randall Klein
    An enchanting look at beautiful Montessori environments
    from around the world and an analysis of how and why
    the basic materials are the same in every school, based on
    the universal needs of body, mind and spirit. The focus
    is on redefining education as spontaneous activities of the
    child rather than what the teacher gives.

Webinar Series: The Power of Montessori—Hope for a New Generation

Bridge to the Peaceful Child
Mary Ellen Maunz and Randall Klein
This webinar is based on Maria Montessori's intriguing teaching on learning to see the child who is not yet there. We explore how we can overcome our hot-button reactions to our children, learn to observe them more carefully, and nurture the concentration that is at the heart of every peaceful child.

Mastery One Step at a Time
Mary Ellen Maunz and Randall Klein
How does a young child learn a complex skill such as writing, reading and understanding the base-ten system of numbers using 1s, 10s, 100s and 1000s in arithmetic? We show you, using a simple principle Maria Montessori called "isolation of difficulty." A logical step-wise approach allows children to succeed at each sub-step of a more complex process, thereby gaining not only knowledge, but also a powerful sense of confidence.

Resources for parents of children and teens

Teaching Your Children Values, Linda and Richard Eyre

The Entitlement Trap: How to Rescue Your Child with a New Family System of Choosing, Earning, and Ownership, Linda and Richard Eyre

7 Habits of Highly Effective Families, Steven Covey

Hold On to Your Kids: Why Parents Need to Matter More Than Peers, Gordon Neufeld and Gabor Maté

Understanding the Human Being: The Importance of the First Three Years of Life, Silvana Quattrocchi Montanaro

Lesson materials and training

The Good Shepherd and the Child: A Joyful Journey,
  Sofia Cavalletti, Patricia Coulter, Gianna Gobbi and
  Silvana Q. Montanaro

Godly Play Resources provides kits with lesson materials for
  the parables, events from the Old and New Testaments
  and lives of the saints. A series of four books by Jerome
  Berryman includes complete instructions for presenting
  the lessons.
  www.godlyplayresources.com
  (800) 445-4390

The Catechesis of the Good Shepherd is an international
  organization which supports the programs of spiritual
  instruction developed by Sofia Cavalletti. The U.S.
  branch provides materials, training and a directory of
  churches where these programs are available.
  www.cgsusa.org
  (708) 524-1210

Notes

Opening quote: Maria Montessori, *Education and Peace* (Washington, D.C.: Henry Regnery, 1972), p. 53.

INTRODUCTION
1. Paul Beyers, "The Spiritual in the Classroom," *Holistic Education Review,* Spring 1992, p. 6.
2. Philip S. Gang, Nina Meyerhof Lynn and Dorothy J. Maver, *Conscious Education: The Bridge to Freedom* (Grafton, Vt.: Daghaz Press, 1992), p. 6.
3. E. M. Standing, *Maria Montessori: Her Life and Work* (New York: Plume, 1998), p. 269.
4. Maria Montessori and E. M. Standing, *The Child in the Church* (St. Paul: Catechetical Guild, 1965), p. 9.
5. Maria Montessori, *The Absorbent Mind* (New York: Henry Holt, 1995), p. 4.

CHAPTER 1
Opening quote: Maria Montessori, *The Secret of Childhood* (Notre Dame, Ind.: Fides Publishing, 1966), p. 41.
1. Jerome W. Berryman, *Teaching Godly Play: How to Mentor the Spiritual Development of Children* (Denver, Col.: Moorehouse Educational Resources, 2009), p. 14.
2. Montessori, *Education and Peace,* p. 43.
3. Maria Montessori, *Spontaneous Activity in Education* (New York: Frederick A. Stokes, 1917), p. 160.
4. Standing, *Maria Montessori: Her Life and Work,* p. 39.
5. Montessori, *The Absorbent Mind,* p. 5.
6. Montessori, *Spontaneous Activity in Education,* p. 192.
7. Maria Montessori, quoted in E. M. Standing, *Maria Montessori: Her Life and Work* (Fresno: Academy Library Guild, 1957), p. 81.
8. Montessori and Standing, *The Child in the Church,* pp. 42–43, 14.

CHAPTER 2
Opening Quote: Montessori, *From Childhood to Adolescence* (New York: Schocken Books, 1948) p. 1.
1. Joan Wester Anderson, *An Angel to Watch Over Me: True Stories of Children's Encounters with Angels* (Chicago: Loyola Press, 2012), pp. 2–4.
2. Ronald Kotulak, *Chicago Tribune,* Special Edition, May 1993, p.1.
3. Ibid, p. 6.
4. Craig Ramey, telephone conversation with the author, 1999.
5. Sofia Cavalletti, *The Religious Potential of the Child: Experiencing*

Scripture and Liturgy with Young Children (Chicago: Liturgy Training Publications, 1992), p. 32.

6. David Dobbs, "Beautiful Teenage Brains," *National Geographic*, 220:4.

7. Just a few of the research findings on the benefits of meditation:

High school students exposed to a relaxation response-based curriculum had significantly increased their self-esteem. (*The Journal of Research and Development in Education*, Volume 27, pp. 226–231, 1994)

Inner city middle school students improved grade score, work habits and cooperation and decreased absences. (*Journal of Research and Development in Education*, Volume 33, pp. 156–165, Spring 2000)

Seventy-eight percent of adolescents who completed an eight-week meditation study reported a reduction in total ADHD symptoms. On neurocognitive test performance, significant improvements were found on the measure of attentional conflict. ("Mindfulness meditation training in adults and adolescents with ADHD," *Journal of Attention Disorders*, Volume 11, pp. 737–746)

Meditation has been found in neurological studies to enhance learners' attention, change their worldviews, and improve communication skills. (A. Jha, J. Krimpinger & M. J. Baime, "Mindfulness training modifies subsystems of attention," *Cognitive, Affective, and Behavioral Neuroscience*, Volume 7, pp. 109–119; P. Grossenbacher, & S. Parkin, "Joining hearts and minds: A contemplative approach to holistic education," *Journal of College & Character*, 7[6]. Retrieved from http://www.kusala.org/pdf/Joining.pdf)

Meditation can increase emotional clarity and sensitivity. (L. Nielsen, & A. W. Kaszniak, "Awareness of subtle emotional feelings: A comparison of long-term meditators and non-meditators," *Emotion*, Volume 6, pp. 392–405)

8. Montessori, *Spontaneous Activity in Education*, p. 168.

9. Cavalletti, *The Religious Potential of the Child*, p. 87.

CHAPTER 3

Opening quote: Personal communication from Dr. Elisabeth Caspari to the author, 1980.

1. The regions of the brain that are most seriously affected by prenatal alcohol exposure in terms of ability to function are the frontal lobes, responsible for judgment and impulse control; the corpus callosum, which coordinates activity in left brain and the right brain (MRI images show that the corpus callosum may be smaller than normal, and in some cases almost nonexistent, in children with fetal alcohol syndrome [FAS]); the hippocampus, which plays a fundamental role in memory, learning, and emotion, the hypothalamus, which controls appetite, emotions, temperature and pain sensation, the cerebellum: controls coordination and movement, behavior and memory; the

basal ganglia, which when damaged affects spatial memory, the perception of time and behaviors like perseveration and the inability to switch modes, work toward goals, predict behavioral outcomes; the amygdala, the central part of emotional circuitry that senses danger, fear and anxiety and plays major role in social behavior, aggression, and emotional memory.

The hypothalamus, amygdala, and hippocampus are part of the limbic system, which regulates emotions, social and sexual behavior, the "fight or flight" response, and empathy, all areas of concern for individuals with prenatal alcohol exposure.

Research by Drs. Clarren and Streissguth shows that alcohol interferes with the migration and organization of brain cells during the first trimester (*Journal of Pediatrics*, Vol. 92(1), 64–67). Heavy drinking during the second trimester, particularly from the tenth to twentieth week after conception, seems to cause more clinical features of FAS than at other times during pregnancy, according to a study in England (*Early Human Development*, 1983 Jul, Vol. 8(2), 99–111.) During the third trimester, the hippocampus is greatly affected, which leads to problems with encoding visual and auditory information, basic skills that are fundamental to reading and math (*Neurotoxicology and Teratology*, 13:357–367, 1991).

Teresa Kellerman, long-time researcher on this devastating issue and Director of the FAS Community Resource Center, explains that one particularly difficult problem with FAS is the gap between the *apparent* ability to function (such as physical appearance and expressive language skills) and the *actual* ability to function (such as social skills, emotional maturity, conscience, abstract reasoning, impulse control and judgment). This gap, according to Kellerman, may be as drastic as a normal looking fifteen-year-old with the social maturity of a five-year-old (fasarizona.com).

2. Helen Wambach, *Life Before Life* (New York: Bantam,1984), p. 120.
3. Ibid., p. 107.
4. Michael Gabriel, *Voices from the Womb* (Lower Lake, Calif.: Aslan Publications, 1992), p. 11.
5. Thomas Verny with John Kelly, *The Secret Life of the Unborn Child* (New York: Dell, 1981), p. 15.
6. In her fascinating book, *Enriching Heredity,* Dr. Marion Diamond, brain researcher at U.C. Berkeley, tells about her experimental work with animals that demonstrates the "lasting effects of both maternal care and enrichment in utero." She states: "To our knowledge, our experiments provide the first evidence that the dimensions of the cerebral cortex [the thinking part of the brain] can be altered ... by enriching the parents before pregnancy and the female during pregnancy." Researchers postulate that the same results might also be obtained with human babies since the basic brain structures of animals are similar to those in man. If this is true, the brain of the newborn can actually be increased in size and complexity by what the

parents do before birth and perhaps even before conception. (Marion Diamond, *Enriching Heredity* [New York: Free Press, 1988], p. 96, quoted in Jane M. Healy, *Endangered Minds: Why Children Don't Think and What We Can Do About It* [New York: Simon & Schuster, 1999], p. 264)

7. For more information about communicating with you unborn baby, see Thomas Verney, *The Secret Life of the Unborn Child.*
8. Mother Teresa, *No Greater Love* (Novato, Calif.: New World Library, 2002), p. 5.

CHAPTER 4

Opening quote: Cavalletti, *The Religious Potential of the Child,* p. 35.

1. Ibid., p. 44.
2. Rainer Maria Rilke, *Letters to a Young Poet,* quoted in Larry Chang, ed., *Wisdom for the Soul: Five Millennia of Prescriptions for Spiritual Healing* (Washington, D.C.: Gnosophia Publishers, 2006), p. 335.
3. David Tame, *The Secret Power of Music* (New York: Destiny books, 1984), p. 136.
4. Clarence Ludlow Brownell, *The Heart of Japan* (London: Methuen, 1904), p. 138.
5. Dorothy Retallack, *The Sound of Music and Plants* (Marina del Rey, Calif: DeVorss & Co., 1973).
6. Colin Rose, *Accelerated Learning* (New York: Dell, 1987), p. 95.
7. Harvey Bird and Gervasia Schreckenberg, *Insight Magazine,* April 4, 1988.
8. Daniel G. Amen, *Making a Good Brain Great: The Amen Clinic Program for Achieving and Sustaining Optimal Mental Performance* (New York: Three Rivers Press, 2005), p. 164.

CHAPTER 5

Opening quote: Ralph Waldo Emerson, *The Conduct of Life* (Boston: Ticknor and Fields, 1860), p. 201.

1. Lawrence Fine, "The Contemplative Practice of Yihudim in Lurianic Kabbalah," in Arthur Green, ed., vol. 14 of *World Spirituality: An Encyclopedic History of the Religious Quest* (New York: Crossroad Publishing Company, 1987), p. 71.
2. Montessori, *The Secret of Childhood,* p. 51.
3. I John 3:11, 4:16.
4. Larry Chang, *Wisdom for the Soul,* p. 355.
5. Fred Eppsteiner, ed., *The Path of Compassion: Writings of Socially Engaged Buddhism,* 2d ed. (Berkeley, Calif.: Parallax Press and Buddhist Peace Fellowship, 1988), p. 19.
6. Karen Armstrong, *A history of God: from Abraham to the Present, the 4000-Year Quest for God* (Portsmouth, NH: Heinemann, 1993) p. 242.
7. Edi Bocelli, quoted in "Famous Blind Tenor Asked for 'Serenity' not His Sight," from http://ministryvalues.com (accessed April 16, 2012).

CHAPTER 6

Opening quote: Montessori, *From Childhood to Adolescence*, p. 24.
 1. Montessori and Standing, *The Child in the Church*, p. 16.
 2. Cavalletti, *The Religious Potential of the Child*, p. 45.
 3. Ibid., p. 47.
 4. Berryman, *Teaching Godly Play*, p. 14.
 5. *Fiery World I* (New York: Agni Yoga Society, 1969), p. 42.

CHAPTER 7

 1. Matt. 13:33.

CHAPTER 8

Opening quote: Cavalletti, *The Religious Potential of the Child*, p. 36.
 1. Maria Montessori, *To Educate the Human Potential* (Oxford: Clio, 1996), p. 16.
 2. Ibid., p. 25.
 3. John Hawkins compiled a book of maxims in French, which was translated into English by his son, Francis, and published with the title *Youths Behaviour, or, Decency in Conversation among Men.* This formed the basis for the list that George Washington wrote at age 16 of 110 "Rules of Civility and Decent Behaviour in Company and Conversation." Biographers regard this list as being formative in the development of his character.

CHAPTER 9

Opening quote: Story summarized from Sr. Maria Antonia, *Under Angel Wings* (Charlotte, N.C.: TAN Books, 2009).
 1. Murray Bodo, *Francis: The Journey and the Dream* (Cincinnati, Ohio: St. Anthony Messenger Press, 1988), p. 8.

CHAPTER 10

Opening quote: Kahlil Gibran, *The Prophet* (New York: Knopf, 1923).
 1. Brother Lawrence, *The Practice of the Presence of God, with Spiritual Maxims* (Grand Rapids, Mich.: Baker Book House, 1967), pp. 12, 30.
 2. Peter L. Benson, Eugene Roehlkepartain and I. Shelby Andress, *Congregations at Crossroads: A National Study of Adults and Youth in the Lutheran Church—Missouri Synod* (Minneapolis, Minn.: Search Institute, 1995), p. 21, quoted in Ben Freudenburg, *The Family Friendly Church* (Loveland, Colo.: Group, 1998), p. 17.
 3. Maria Montessori, *Childhood Education* (Chicago: Regnery, 1974), p. 13.
 4. Montessori, *The Secret of Childhood* (New York: Ballantine Books, 1972), p. 7.
 5. William Wordsworth, "The Rainbow."
 6. Maria, *The Secret of Childhood*, p. 149.
 7. Montessori, *Spontaneous Activity in Education*, p. 194.
 8. Maria Montessori, *The Child in the Family* (Chicago: Regnery, 1970), p. 120.
 9. Montessori, *The Absorbent Mind*, p. 285.

About the Author

Mary Ellen Maunz, mother of three grown children, has forty years of experience in Montessori education as an early childhood and elementary teacher, administrator and teacher educator. She holds a M.Ed. in Integrative Learning with an emphasis on Montessori from Endicott College and a B.S. in Child Development from the University of La Verne. She holds credentials as a Montessori teacher for ages 2½ to 7 from the Association Montessori Internationale (AMI), for ages 6 to 12 from the Pan-American Montessori Society (PAMS) and as a Master Teacher from PAMS.

Mary Ellen was fortunate to work for twenty-three years with Dr. Elisabeth Caspari, a student and personal friend of Dr. Maria Montessori. She served for nearly ten years as a Board Member and Commissioner for the Montessori Accreditation Council for Teacher Education (MACTE) and continues to act as onsite evaluator for teacher education programs.

She has a certificate of Pastoral Care from Houston's Institutes of Religion, where she studied the Catechesis of the Good Shepherd with Dr. Sofia Cavalletti. Following this training she established a specially prepared or atrium environment and taught in her Sunday school for more than twenty years.

Mary Ellen founded a Montessori teacher education institution in Saint Petersburg, Russia, where she teaches every summer. She is also the founder and Program Director of Age of Montessori, an organization that provides online and in-person training in early childhood education. Through Age of Montessori, she continues to spread the authentic original method and message of Maria Montessori. She cordially invites you to visit her website at www.ageofmontessori.org.

Made in the USA
Lexington, KY
12 September 2012